CYBERBULLYING

BREAKING THE CYCLE OF CONFLICT

DR. PAUL MILLER

CYBERBULLYING
BREAKING THE CYCLE OF CONFLICT

A Qualitative Study of Black Female Experiences
with Cyberbullying in an Urban Environment

CHALFANT ECKERT

PUBLISHING

Library of Congress Control Number: 2015960704

ISBN: 978-1-63308-203-8 (hardback)
         978-1-63308-204-5 (paperback)
         978-1-63308-205-2 (ebook)

Cover and Interior Design by R'tor John D. Maghuyop

CHALFANT ECKERT
PUBLISHING

1028 S Bishop Avenue, Dept. 178
Rolla, MO 65401

Printed in United States of America

Submitted in partial fulfillment
of the requirements for the degree
Ed.D. in Executive Leadership

Supervised by
Dr. Jeannine Dingus-Eason

Committee Member
Dr. Ruth Harris

Ralph C. Wilson, Jr. School of Education
St. John Fisher College

December 2011

CONTENTS

DEDICATION

This work is dedicated to my loving wife Latoya and two amazing children, Amya, 10 and Paul (PJ), 5. I could not have completed this journey without their love and support. I embarked this daunting task of completing a doctorate to show my kids; if I can do it, so can you, anyone can, if they work hard enough. My wife has endured my absence due to the fact that I had to read, write, and conduct research instead of being a full-time dad. It takes a special woman to be there until the end. I'd like to thank my Grandparents because I would not have ever gone to college, if not for their influence, and my mom for raising me into who I have become. Additionally, I hope this work and completion of this process are examples for my younger sister and others to use education as their guide to achieving excellence. Lastly, I'd like to thank my Aunt Sheila Stanley for helping me out; I would not have even made it through the doors of Fisher's Ed.D program without you.

Full acknowledgment must be given to my dissertation committee, Dr. Jeannine Dingus-Eason and Dr. Ruth Harris. I would not have been able to complete this process without their wisdom and guidance. They instilled an astute level of understanding and respect for receiving a doctorate by demanding a relentless level of excellence. What doesn't kill you will make you stronger! Additionally, I would like to acknowledge my Executive Mentors, Dr. Cheryl Holloway, and Dr. Jim Colt. Both individuals were patient and provided me with tools I needed to successfully complete this process.

BIOGRAPHICAL SKETCH

Paul Miller was born and raised in Rochester, NY. He attended RCSD schools and is a successful survivor of Rochester's inclement, impoverished living conditions. It has ameliorated him into a strong confident and competent leader. He believes that he is a role model in every facet of his life. Paul demonstrates his competency as a role model by having strong morals and values, and a passion for education.

Paul Miller is a doctoral candidate at St. John Fisher College. He received a Bachelor's of Science in Physical Education and Teacher Certification from SUNY Brockport in 2000, and a Master's in Educational Administration in 2005 from St. John Fisher College. Throughout his 12 years in the field of education, he has served as an Elementary Physical Education Teacher and as an Assistant Principal for grades 7-12 in the Rochester City School District. Additionally, Paul is the Director of Operations for Team E Foundation, a non-for- profit organization that's primary mission is to provide college scholarships to inner-city youth who deserve second chances.

Upon entering the Ed.D program in Executive Leadership at St. John Fisher, Paul studied executive leadership and conducted comprehensive research on collaboration, teamwork, analysis of data, and laws, policy and procedures. Under the guidance of his dissertation chair, Dr. Jeannine Dingus-Eason and committee member Dr. Ruth Harris, Paul conducted a qualitative study on the experiences Black adolescent females have with cyberbullying in an urban high school environment.

ABSTRACT

This study examines and analyzes the effects of cyberbullying among Black adolescent females in an urban setting. This population is largely excluded from Digital Youth Culture (DYC) research within cyberbullying literature (Patchin & Hinduja, 2006), even though such research is clearly warranted. To understand school violence, students must be viewed as social actors, experiencing the negative ramifications of DYC in school.

These ramifications result from an imbalance of power generated through the use of aggressive tactics designed to damage a teen's reputation, social status, and emotional well-being. Currently, no research reports how cyberbullying manifests itself in an urban context, among Black females online and in school (Hinduja & Patchin, 2008). This study examined cyberbullying, categorized as disrespect online, and how it occurs among urban Black females. This qualitative, phenomenological study, employed four data gathering techniques: a) demographic profile sheets; b) semi-structured interviews; c) field notes; and, d) document collection. The four forms of data were interwoven and assisted in exploring cyberbullying, relational aggression, and conflict among the study's participants.

The findings identified four relevant themes in terms of online identity, underdeveloped relationships, conflict, and conflict resolution. The four emergent themes are: a) Facebook Thuggin; b) Moving Too Fast; c) You Gonna Have to See Me; and d) Who Barks the Loudest. The interrelated findings clarify how urban Black adolescent females experience cyberbullying. This study is designed to assist educators with teaching Black females how to manage conflict without sacrificing social status or the perception of respect.

CHAPTER 1

INTRODUCTION

A significant result of the digitization of society has been the increase in cyberbullying, a 21st-century form of bullying among teenagers. Cyberbullying is characterized as threats and/or harassment carried out through electronic devices by an individual or group (Mason, 2008; Beasley, 2004). It inflicts mental anguish upon its victims but rarely progresses to face-to-face conflicts (Juvonen & Gross, 2008). Current research espouses that cyberbullying is typically more common among females (Lenhart, 2007). Online aggression between females has become part of the Digital Youth Culture (DYC), but inattention has been provided to urban adolescent Black females within the DYC. This population has not been the focus of DYC research within the cyberbullying literature (Patchin & Hinduja, 2006), even though research is warranted because of the frequency that cyberbullying occurs among teens ages 12-17.

Contrary to this research, education practitioners see the physical manifestation of cyberbullying incidents during school (Colt, 2009). Unfortunately, the No Child Left Behind Act does not mandate that schools provide insight as to why violent incidents occur (Gooden & Harrington, 2005), but only report that an incident did occur. Thus, providing a need to further understand the experiences Black adolescent females have incurred with cyberbullying to ultimately learn how it affected the urban school environment. The example below provides insight into how cyberbullying generates conflict, specifically among young Blacks in an urban environment.

NARRATIVE OF CYBERBULLYING IN AN URBAN SCHOOL CONTEXT

During the 2009-2010 school year, two students at Monticello High School, a large, predominately Black, inner-city high school in upstate New York, began a tumultuous relationship. Kayla, an outgoing Black female in her junior year, found herself drawn to her classmate, Mark, a 17-year-old Black male. After affirming his love and adoration for Kayla publicly, Mark secretly flirted with other girls and began dating a scrappy 17-year-old named Jackie, who often presented disciplinary challenges for school administrators.

As Mark and Jackie's relationship progressed, Kayla and Mark grew apart. Mark started sneaking off school grounds to spend time with Jackie. The pair also connected daily through social networking on FaceBook and MySpace. Rumors eventually reached Kayla via school and MySpace, but she refused to believe that Mark was "hooking up with another girl." Mark was Kayla's first sexual partner, and she was fiercely loyal, defending Mark against anyone who questioned his virtue. However, everyone around Kayla could see that Mark treated her poorly.

Eventually, Kayla overheard classmates commenting on Jackie's MySpace page, where she alluded to secret hook-ups between herself and Mark. In retaliation, Kayla posted derogatory comments about Jackie on her MySpace page, even threatening bodily harm The two young ladies partook in acts of cyberbullying such as trying to defame one another, in order to one-up each other in front of a community of viewers composed of their peers. Kayla attempted to post comments directly on Jackie's page, but Jackie deleted her as a friend and blocked Kayla from her page. Daily, both girls employed cyberbullying, delivering negative, hurtful comments via cyberspace. The negative comments soon surfaced at school via spectators and began to create disruptions, due to the fact that most students were focused on trying to see a fight instead of school work. In one incident, the girls were reprimanded by the school administration for cursing at each other in the hallway because they were frustrated with the computer acting as their shield. Unimpeded, the situation seemed destined for physical conflict. Fortunately, school administration intervened, and all parties were sent home to calm down and asked to return the following day for mediation.

School administration obtained a copy of the ongoing Internet feud from Kayla's MySpace page and informed everyone involved that if the feud transcended cyberspace and resulted in a fight at school, students would face a long-term suspension (for a period greater than 5 days) and, potentially, an arrest. Even though multiple mediations and warnings were given, incidents kept occurring. The situation escalated to the point that Kayla finally challenged Jackie to fight her at Kayla's home. Jackie saw the message via MySpace and alerted Mark through a text message. Jackie, Mark, and several other relatives sent a message that they were on their way to Kayla's house. Kayla and her large family were ready. Jackie and her crew arrived, and fists, bats, tennis rackets and knives were used to inflict pain in a violent altercation. Kayla's mother chased after Mark with a tennis racket, and her step-father, armed with a machete, went searching for him. Everyone escaped the fray with only minimal injuries.

Once alerted, an administrator set up in-school mediation, in the hopes of preventing similar physical altercations for the remainder of the school year. Understanding how immense the Internet's role was in enhancing an already tense situation, helped school administration defuse future situations.

In this instance, cyberbullying transcended cyberspace, injecting violent behavior into the school environment. The feud between the two young urban adolescent Black females began in cyberspace, a virtual, public place where all of their cyberfriends could witness the event. In defense, each girl responded to the other's perceived disrespect, as both felt it necessary to save face with peers and earn back any lost respect through physical violence (Jones, 2004). Cyberspace provided a forum to fan the flame of conflict in front of a large audience. In years preceding the Internet, conflict could be perpetuated through telephone calls, which limited the number of spectators and, as a result, provided a slower forum for spreading conflict (McQuade, Colt, & Meyer, 2009). With technological advances and the widespread use of social networking as a public forum, cyberbullying has become a major problem.

STATEMENT OF THE RESEARCH PROBLEM

The aforementioned narrative describes a real-life incident in which cyberbullying transcended cyberspace and evolved into violence within a school context. Current research on cyberbullying states that Internet conflict does not typically escalate to face-to-face conflict (Hinduja & Patchin, 2008). Yet, the previous anecdote illustrates how two urban Black adolescent girls reacted in response to cyberbullying. Unfortunately, there is limited research devoted to examining cyberbullying and its effect in an urban school environment among adolescent Black females, because most of the contemporary research explores cyberbullying among populations of predominantly White adolescent females in suburban and rural environments (Li, 2005; Lenhart, Madden, & Hitlin, 2005; Li, 2006; Hinduja & Patchin, 2007). Thus, the researcher has observed a need to further understand the experiences of urban adolescent Black females in relation to cyberbullying. This qualitative study asks urban adolescent Black females about their perceptions and experiences with cyberbullying in an attempt to understand whether cyberbullying can be linked to in-school conflict. The following section will explain the frequency in which urban school violence occurs. Additionally formulating an argument which articulates that school violence data does not clearly indicate why incidents occur, nor does it disaggregate by race and gender combined, with a specific interest in Black females. To omit such data does a disservice and pays an inattention to understanding the experiences urban Black adolescent females have as participants and victims of school violence.

URBAN SCHOOL VIOLENCE: AN ASSESSMENT OF CURRENT SCHOOL DATA

Under No Child Left Behind, public schools are federally mandated to report data on violent incidents and nonfatal crimes that occur on and around school grounds (National Center for Education Statistics [IES], 2010). In 2002, the federal government mandated that state education agencies (SEAs) and local education agencies (LEAs) develop policies and procedures to deal with persistently dangerous schools (Gooden & Harrington, 2005). The legislation gave little to no guidance to the states in terms of the criteria used to determine a persistently dangerous school; a disparity which impedes accurate measurement.

Even if data is collected consistently at the school and district level, it is not necessarily compiled yearly on a national level. Statistics from 2007 show that 1.5 million youth between the ages of 12-18 self-report as victims of nonfatal crimes at school (IES, 2010). In 2008, 47 of every 1000 students were victims of non-fatal crimes. There were four fatal crimes per 1000 students aged 12-18 and eight percent of 9-12 grade students experienced being threatened with a weapon at school in 2008 (IES). Urban schools, in particular, report that in 2008, approximately 78 percent of the registered violent crimes (school violence, weapons, crime, and bullying) occurred in urban schools. During the 2007-2008 school year, 36 percent of urban schools reported 20 or more violent incidents (IES). Unfortunately, reports filed in urban schools in response to violent incidents do not typically include explanations as to what inspired the violent acts or other factors that may have contributed to the in-school violence.

Locally and nationally the absence of understanding the motives as to why individuals partake in violent acts at school can hinder advancement of violence prevention strategies (Astor, Benbenishty, & Estrada, 2009). For example, in 2004-2005, New York State classified 92 of its public schools as "persistently dangerous" or as a "school in need of being watched" (National Center for Statistics, 2002). In an effort to isolate trends, schools track criminal activities such as homicide, sexual offenses, assault, and use or threatened use of a weapon (National Center for Statistics). According to these reports, violent incidents most frequently occur in classrooms, offices, hallways, on school grounds, or in the parking lot (Shelton et al., p. 25). The New York State school districts are mandated to report the incidents but are not provided with clear guidelines as to how the implementation of violence prevention strategies should occur (New York State Education Department [NYSED], 2010). Each district is individually responsible for figuring out why violent incidents occur and for implementing appropriate strategies. Nationally and on a district level there is no clear understanding as to why violent incidents occur and exactly who is the population committing the violent occurrences.

The federal government does not require data disaggregation specific to the race and gender of students involved in violent incidents, even though such data is readily available (Gooden & Harrington, 2005). Such disregard for detail is problematic, as schools are not otherwise motivated to analyze which populations of students are creating the problems. Such analysis could guide schools toward the development of specific and appropriate interventions, in response to the unique socio-emotional needs of adolescent males and females, respectively (Rice & Dolgin, 2008). For example, there are national statistics which indicate that Blacks account for 38 percent of reported school violence, but the report does not identify why the violence occurred or the gender of the people involved in the incident (School Violence, Weapons, Crime, and Bullying, 2010). Alarmingly, such reporting clearly displays a high rate of incidents occurring among Black youth without further identifying more specific trends such as common motivations for violence or whether those involved are most often male or female. In terms of gender, 26 percent of females between 12-17 years old report being engaged in violent activities at school and other places (School Violence, Weapons, Crime, and Bullying,

2010). Additionally, 18.6 percent specifically admit to being involved in severe fights. Severe fights are not clearly defined, but the term implies that the altercation resulted in some form of physical injury.

The data shows that violent incidents occur at an alarming rate. More specifically, and at a higher rate than males, females report that they are afraid to go to school (IES, 2010). To further illuminate this idea, violence is not limited to a crime committed against an individual, it also refers to bullying. Bullying often acts as a gateway to more severe crimes, with violent behaviors such as carrying weapons, fighting, and inflicting and sustaining injuries from fighting are closely related to bullying (Nansel et al., 2001). Bullying can often be an indicator, potentially revealing a pattern that leads to more criminal behavior (Olweus, 1999). In 2007, 33 percent of female students reported being bullied at school, with five percent citing cyberbullying specifically (IES, 2010); far exceeding the statistics of their male counterparts in both instances. Of the individuals who reported being cyberbullied, 73 percent identified the cyberbullying as a recurring event.

The literature on urban school violence and cyberbullying has commonalities because they both pay an inattention to specifically understanding the roles Black females play. What remains unknown are the rates of violence among urban Black female students and what motivates their participation in violent acts and/or victimization at school (Elliot, 1994). While data on cyberbullying is now being collected, this information needs greater aggregation in terms of race and gender in order to get a better picture of who participates in and who is victimized by cyberbullying, and why.

Cyberbullying· digital divide. This section will address cyberbullying as a significant part of the Digital Youth Culture, which affects most teens (Lenhart, 2007), but does not devote attention specifically how it affects urban Black adolescent females. Cyberbullying has been studied for approximately 10 years with some assumptions made on the part of researchers with respect to those who participate in cyberbullying and others who are impacted by acts of cyberbullying in the school environment. For example, Patchin and Hinduja (2006) highlighted in their research, that cyberbullying is a problem more closely associated with affluent suburbs and Caucasian females.

This monolithic approach has been categorized throughout the literature as a digital divide that causes minorities to have limited access to the Internet; therefore, a limited need to study that population has developed. Many researchers have conducted research on cyberbullying with demographics of up to 80 percent White females (Caravan 2006; Epstein & Kazmierczack, 2007; and Lenhart, Madden, Macgill, & Smith, 2007). An overwhelming overt inattention to other ethnic group's involvement with cyberbullying creates an assumption which indicates similar outcomes and experiences occur from being cyberbullied. A recent study reveals that Blacks have access to the Internet, but no discourse was provided about their experiences (Pew Research Center, 2010).

According to Pew Research Center, a study conducted in 2010 shows that Blacks connect to the Internet through multiple means including their mobile phones. The research has not explained the sudden shift. However, in the past year, the rate of Blacks who own laptops has risen from 34 to 51 percent. Additionally, households that make less than $30,000 have increased their Internet usage from 35 to 46 percent in the past year. The study shows that the affluent have more access to the Internet than their lower-class counterparts, but almost 50 percent of individuals who only graduated high school have access to the Internet (Pew Research Center, 2010). The Pew Study encourages additional study of cyberbullying among urban minorities in order to understand some important implications that were not previously examined. Information about the implications of cyberbullying among Black youth, especially Black females, is lacking. As a result, this current study will explore, from a Black female's perspective, the ways cyberbullying impacted their urban high school experience. When cyberbullying occurs in this type of public display, there is little known about the results it will produce among Black adolescent females in an urban setting. The following section will examine the role that social networking plays as the platform for cyberbullying among females and implications will be made as to how it has the potential to materialize in the urban school environment, thus, having potential to explain why some violent incidents occur.

Social networking as a cyberbullying platform for adolescent girls. Social networking is a popular pastime that increases access to one's peers which, when coupled with a lack of online supervision, freely facilitates cyberbullying. Individuals who partake in social networking do so for various reasons. According to Surra and Milardo (1991), social networking opens up opportunities for interplay among people who have similar past and present experiences and relationships. Adolescent females, specifically, express an innate need to form relationships, which is crucial to the adolescent female's identity and maturation process (Rice & Dolgin, 2008). As females in grades seven through twelve develop and search for their identity, aspects of the school environment may impact this internal journey through peer pressure and the desire to "fit in" with certain groups in school. Girls, additionally, try to "fit in" online, as their online identity, social networking page, and netspeak vocabulary must meet the expectations of online peers (McQuade et al., 2009).

Subsequently, the Internet and use of technology have become part of teenage identity, as those born after 1990 are commonly referred to as members of the Digital Youth Culture (DYC). The regular use of the Internet by teens in some cases averages between six to nine hours a day amplifying the child's need to be socially accepted (Berson, Berson, & Ferron, 2002) because the online community mirrors the regular world. For example, cliques formed at school are reinforced on social networking sites, perpetuating a new forum for bullying (Hinduja & Patchin, 2008).

Due to the evolution of sharing social spaces through Internet usage, social networking has become one of the primary platforms for cyberbullying (Lenhart et al., 2007). Social networking can support positive and negative motivations. While some seek to connect or reconnect with friends in spite of vast distances, others use social networking sites to propagate rumors heard in social settings such as school. When rumors start in a school building, the social networking site provides an outlet for rumors to grow and spread vastly at speeds that could not be achieved without Internet access (Hinduja & Patchin, 2008).

Before the Internet, students could go home and escape the social pressures of school. In cyberspace, however, peer-pressure is not limited to the confines of one school building but includes youth from across the world. Adolescence is already known as a time of elevated psychological risk due to an underdeveloped sense of self (Brown & Gilligan, 1992). The vulnerability experienced during this time period is exacerbated when adolescents struggle to understand who they are and who they want to become, are projected into cyberspace. Social networking is important to adolescent development as it represents an evolution of social space where adolescents convene and rally for popularity and social status. When cyberbullying occurs on the social networks, it can add stress and pressure to the lives of adolescents already facing the challenges of maturation (Gross, 2004).

Previously, high school was the primary social space where relationships with peers were formed and broken. McClung (2006) advises that girls experience high school as a breeding ground for broken relationships due to pressure from large populations, boys, and self-imposed identity issues. High school is a subculture in which many of these relationships are formed. As relationships form, a sense of class inclusion is fostered. Cliques occur when people seek out relationships from a higher social status in order to elevate their perceived class status among their peers (Rice & Dolgin, 2008). A teen's social self is what he or she thinks others see which has the potential to affect what others think as well (Rice & Dolgin, 2008). Being popular and socially successful can elevate an individual's social class and can increase an adolescent's ability to remain un-bullied. In an effort to establish a persona, the adolescent develops an "*ideal self*," who the individual would like to be (Rice & Dolgin, 2008).

If the adolescent is not part of the popular clique or does not have the ability to develop a persona that emanates confidence, an imbalance of power can occur which may often result in bullying. In order for bullying to take place, a social place of interaction is needed. Previously, social interaction took place by face-to-face encounters, but the fact that 90 percent of 12-17-year-olds go online regularly has caused frequent social interaction and bullying to occur on social networking sites such as FaceBook and MySpace (Lenhart, 2006; Hinduja & Patchin, 2008). The online conflict is referred to as cyberbullying.

Researchers suggest that cyberbullying has the potential to cause incidents to occur at school. For example, Colt (2009) surveyed over 100 school administrators, 74 percent of whom said that cyberbullying occurred outside of school more often. Yet, evidence suggests that incidents on school property have a direct correlation to cyberbullying. Studies dated before 2006 often recognized emails, text, chat rooms, and IM's as the most prevalent spaces in which cyberbullying could occur (National i-SAFE Survey, 2004).

Not only is viewing adolescent development important for understanding why youth participate in social networking, but it is also helpful to understand why conflict occurs in social spaces. Some who have not previously acquired elite social status may achieve it due to an ability to position themselves properly in cyberspace. The digital youth culture provides opportunities for adolescents to use cyberspace as a way to develop their social identity and possibly disguise their in-person persona (McQuade, Colt, & Meyer, 2009). The Internet levels the playing field for many socially awkward individuals because they can be whoever they want to be, as anonymity provides the opportunity for adolescents to experiment with their identity (Calvert, 2002).

Relational aggression will be explained and used as the theoretical framework, which bridges the literature on the Digital Youth Culture (DYC), social status, identity, and school violence. Social networking is now a space where relationships are formed and can inspire either an elevation or decline in social status (Hinduja & Patchin, 2008). Relationships and social status can be negatively infringed upon, which may create conflict through the use of relational aggression.

RELATIONAL AGGRESSION AS A THEORETICAL FRAMEWORK

The Internet is a venue which allows people to connect with one another, establish relationships, communicate with the masses, but there can be a dark side as well. Communication and relationships can be damaged quicker than they were established. This is often due to relational aggression, a disguised and manipulative aggression that is designed to affect another person's social status and relationships (Xie, Farmer, & Cairns, 2003). Girls, especially, express an innate need to establish connections with others socially (Brown & Gilligan, 1992). The desire to fulfill this need often leads girls to become victims of emotional attack. Feeling vulnerable often causes girls to overcompensate by guarding themselves at all times. They do so by forming cliques, tearing down others, abandoning friends, and exposing confidences (Nicklin, n.d.). Often, aggression involves a physical and/or verbal exchange.

Relational aggression manifests itself through cyberbullying, a form of using overt and covert tactics to damage someone else emotionally and socially. Typically, this form of aggression manifests itself in shared social spaces where girls gather to form cliques (Simmons, 2002). Previously, relational aggression was limited to public places such as school. However, due to the influence of the Digital Youth Culture (DYC), relational aggression is additionally situated in cyberspace, more specifically during online social networking (McQuade et al., 2009). As technology such as iPhones and other all-in-one portable devices emerge rapidly through society, patrons are able to exchange data and communicate all the time. The DYC encourages this generation to come-of-age with one another and share their attitudes, feelings, and life experiences through communication and data-enabled devices (McQuade et al.). Girls, as participants in DYC, can utilize social networking, texting, and tweeting as weapons against each other's social status.

Intentionally affecting an individual's social status is a misuse of power (Olweus, 1994). Cyberbullying and traditional bullying use power differently, as traditional bullying supports strength, power, physical prowess, while cyberbullying is more cerebral, employing quick wit, cleverness, and computer proficiency skills (Hinduja & Patchin, 2007). Conflict can occur in social spaces among adolescents because of the continuous quest for power and social status and the importance of forming relationships (Rice & Dolgin, 2008). This form of relational aggression can cause mental anguish at school, which can significantly affect students. Not only is it a form of mental anguish, but it can be categorized as a form of abusive violence (Baldry, 2004).

Expanding the conversation, Baldry (2004) suggests that relational aggression causes depression, anxiety, and withdrawal due to actions that represent exclusion, contamination of a person's social status, dissemination of lies about a person, and manipulation of the truth about someone's actions or character. Even though relational aggression has the potential to exude detrimental outcomes, Dellasega and Nixon (2003) suggest it is harder to distinguish these covert tactics, in comparison to more physically aggressive methods. An example of a covert tactic is if a female blocks someone from viewing their social networking page, and then they post negative comments about the blocked individual so that individual cannot witness the defaming. Very often mutual friends are still able to view the comments, and the promulgation of rumors begins with the potential to cause conflict.

Acts of relational aggression in the form of cyberbullying can damage relationships quickly due to the speed in which information is passed and the large amount of people who can access information. The Internet has become a social microcosm based on society in which social isolation can be damaging as well, due to a limited network of friends. The effects of relational aggression on girls may linger and inhibit future relationships as well (Owens, Shute, & Slee, 2000). For example, friendships among girls are frequently based on trust, intimacy, and self-disclosure (McClung, 2006). Such relationships require time to develop and cause the participants to become vulnerable to relational aggression (Owens et al., 2000). Over time, the potential for bullying increases. Adolescent girls let their guards down and give their friends unfettered access to their most personal secrets and thoughts (Rice & Dolgin, 2008). This personal information is easily converted into ammunition used to harm individuals emotionally by damaging their social status.

Using violent, relational aggressive tactics instead of actual physical violence, allows girls to maintain social distinction. The social distinction of being a lady in public is important, as participation in physical violence can be viewed as tangible evidence, damaging to a lady's reputation, whereas relational aggression is generally behind the scenes (Baldry, 2004). Traditionally, a girl is told to conduct herself "like a lady" and to display outward physical aggression contradicts this imposed societal standard. Relational aggression manifested through cyberbullying, enables girls to fight without the use of direct physical contact (Gonick, 2004). In order to maintain a lady-like reputation, girls often choose to avoid physical altercations. According to Underwood (2003), girls manifest their aggression indirectly by adopting social and relational aggressive techniques. For example, a girl might exemplify such aggression by spreading a rumor on the Internet about another girl. Gonick (2004) suggests that boys' physically aggressive behaviors are healthy, whereas girls' use of manipulation can be psychologically harmful.

The research does not discern whether relational aggression has the potential to damage females differently based on ethnicity. Relational aggression is an equal opportunity form of oppression, but this study will explore whether cyberbullying converges and creates conflict within an urban school environment among Black adolescent females, by studying their experiences with participation and victimization. According to Anderson (1999), relational aggression among Black adolescent females has the potential to converge into violent face-to-face conflicts due to the importance of maintaining respectful relationships. The urban school violence literature does not give discourse to this notion and therefore, a limited understanding is had as to why and what causes urban Black adolescent females to partake in violence (Bennet-Johnson, 2004). Thus, establishing an importance of learning how relational aggression in the form of cyberbullying affects adolescent Black females in an urban school environment. The following section will pontificate how relational aggression has to potential to manifest itself between urban adolescent Black females.

Urban black adolescent females and relational aggression. Black urban youth may respond differently to an aggressive situation due to consistent exposure to adverse living conditions, as opposed to the literature on cyberbullying proclaiming that this form of relational aggression does not generally end in face-to-face conflict. Many urban Black youth have an ingrained value of respect that becomes a micro-system of their socialization (Deutsch & Jones, 2008). Approximately 70 percent of urban Black youth live in neighborhoods associated with poverty and violence (USDHHS, 2001). Herrenkohl et al. (2001) warn that Black youth are exposed to violence in their communities, offered inadequate support, denied academic and economic building opportunities, and, as such, are more likely to respond violently in adverse situations.

Adolescence is already a time of uncertainty, but when coupled with historical injustice of oppression and adverse living conditions, discernable outcomes may occur when faced with difficult situations involving aggression. Gonick (2004) characterizes adolescence as a time when young women feel they can only count on themselves and when any vulnerability can provoke social anxieties about the world in which they must survive. When threats are made to an urban adolescent Black girl's vulnerability, her response has the potential to escalate to verbal and physical aggression for the purpose of re-establishing lost respect. Among urban city residents, respect may be valuable as or more than money. According to Anderson (1999), respect is viewed as social capital, which is highly valued because other forms of capital may be obsolete. The origination of respect as a theory among inner city residents has materialized from a distrust of the criminal justice system. The belief is that there are two criminal justice systems; one for black and a different one for whites (Anderson). This view has created a version of justice interpreted by some inner city blacks as a "perversion of the Golden Rule" (Anderson, p. 68). Doing on to others as you want to be done to self; in the urban setting can be referred to as retribution.

If an urban Black female allows herself to be disrespected it could cause her to lose social status. Miller (2008) describes disrespect among urban Black females as a possible safety hazard. The loss of social status creates an opportunity to be preyed upon, because of the appearance of being weak (Anderson, 1999). Among urban Black females, a need to save face in public places, like school, or even over the Internet may be very important. One way that respect may be re-established is by fighting and winning the physical altercation; another way is for the individual to present themselves as verbally tougher (Anderson 1999; Jones, 2004; Miller, 2008).

When relational aggression in the form cyberbullying, also categorized as disrespect online, occurs among urban Black youth, limited research examines how it manifests itself in social contexts or how it may be distressing Black youth. The following research questions will guide this study to learn about urban Black adolescent's female's experiences as victims and participants in cyberbullying.

RESEARCH QUESTION

The following research questions will guide this qualitative study in an effort to determine what cyberbullying looks like when it occurs among Black females in an urban environment. The study will also attempt to lend understanding how it converges from cyberspace to create conflict in the urban school environment. This research will address one main question and one sub-question:

1. *How do urban Black adolescent females describe their experiences as participants and victims of cyberbullying?*

    1a. If they were victimized, what were their experiences?

Studying cyberbullying, specific to Black adolescent females in an urban environment, is a newer phenomenon. The phenomenon will be illustrated with Black adolescent females' experiences with cyberbullying and their perceived experiences of victimization. This question will guide the study to provide understanding about this phenomenon.

DEFINITION OF TERMS

Black - A person having origins in any of the Black racial groups of Africa. It includes people who indicate their race as "Black, African American., or Negro,"(US Census Bureau, 2000, ¶ 4).

Blog - An interactive web journal or diary, the contents of which are posted online and viewable by some or all individuals (Patchin & Hinduja, 2005; Colt, 2009, p. 12).

Bullying - A type of aggression in which (a) the behavior is deliberate and harmful, (b) the behavior is repeated over time, and (c) there is an imbalance of power involving the more powerful attacking the less powerful (Nansel et al., 2001; Colt, 2009, p. 12).

Chat - An online conversation typically carried out by people who use nicknames instead of their real names. You can read messages from others in the chat room and type and send in a message or reply (Patchin & Hinduja, 2005; Colt, 2009, p. 12).

Conflict - To come into collision or disagreement; be contradictory, at variance, or in opposition; clash (Dictionary.com, 2011).

Cyberbullying - Willful and repeated harm inflicted through the medium of electronic text (Patchin & Hinduja, 2006; Colt, 2009, p. 12).

Cyberspace - The electronic universe created by computer networks in which individuals socially interact (Patchin & Hinduja, 2005; Colt, 2009, p. 12).

Digital Youth Culture - A computerized and technology-based society that supports social conditions (Sampat & McQuade, 2008).

E-mail - Electronic mail that allows Internet users to send and receive electronic text to and from other Internet users (Patchin & Hinduja, 2005; Colt, 2009, p. 12).

Instant Messaging (IM) - Private, real-time communications with anyone on a contact or buddy list (Willard, 2006; Colt, 2009, p. 14).

Internet - A worldwide network of computers communicating with each other via phone lines, satellite links, wireless networks, and cable systems (Patchin & Hinduja, 2005; Colt, 2009, p. 14).

Relational Aggression - Relational aggression is disguised, manipulative aggression geared toward affecting one's social status and relationships (Xie, Farmer, & Cairns, 2003).

Social Networking Site - Web-based services that allow individuals to construct a profile, share information with other users, and view lists of others made by other users within the system (Boyd, 2007; Colt, 2009, p. 15).

Violence - Violence for these purposes may be defined as poor treatment due to action, treatment, or physical force (Violence, 2010).

CHAPTER SUMMARY

This study will examine how cyberbullying affects Black adolescent females in an urban setting, such as school. When cyberbullying occurs among urban Black youth as a form of relational aggression, no research is currently done to report how it manifests itself in social contexts or how it may distress Black youth.

Chapter 2 is a selective literature review that focuses on the accumulated empirical data surrounding cyberbullying, scholarly literature on urban school violence, and relational aggression. An analysis and synthesis of the literature will occur throughout chapter two. Chapter 3 discusses how the supporting methodology is designed and conducted with the goal of answering specific research questions designed to provide understanding into the experiences that cyberbullying may have among Black females. Chapter 4 will provide the findings which derived from the research, and Chapter 5 will illuminate implications and recommendations that directly developed from the findings.

CHAPTER 2

LITERATURE REVIEW

Chapter 2 represents a selective overview of the literature on urban schools, cyberbullying, and relational aggression that will illuminate the need to conduct further research to understand the experiences of urban adolescent Black females in relation to cyberbullying, and how it is currently unknown how it evolves in the school environment. Also missing from our understanding of school violence from both mandated state reports and social science research on schools is an examination of students as social actors who experience the negative ramifications of Digital Youth Culture (DYC) on their school experiences.

Cyberbullying has the potential to cause adolescents distress at school and affects their identity development, especially females because of the frequency with which they access the Internet and their tendency to form significant social relationships on-line (Juvonen & Gross, 2008). Acts of relational aggression online, or cyberbullying, can adversely affect relationships quickly because of the speed that information is transmitted and because of the large number of people who have access to the information. Currently, the literature does not unearth how cyberbullying affects populations in an urban school environment, specifically adolescent Black females (Wollack & Mitchell, 2000; Li, 2006; Lenhart, Madden, Macgill, & Smith, 2007).

URBAN SCHOOL ENVIRONMENT

This selective review of urban school violence literature will divulge that student's perceptions are a good indicator to create violence prevention programs. This portion of the literature will additionally focus on the need for school administration to focus on patterns of behavior, which can be done by establishing a good connection with students and the community (Renfro, Huebner, Callahan, & Ritchey, 2003). The urban school violence literature establishes a connection with this original study's proposed methodologies by extenuating the importance of understanding student's perceptions and experience with urban school conflict, even though it is not a nationally accepted practice.

Many urban schools face problems that have the ability to negatively affect student's achievement and behavior. Some of the problems that currently exist within urban schools are bullying, harassment, discipline problems, gang membership, drugs and alcohol, and high dropout rates (Renfro, Huebner, Callahan, & Ritchey, 2003). The aforementioned problems have become progressively worse over the past decade. In 1998 students age 12 to 18 were victims to 253,000 non-fatal, but violent crimes, whereas, in 2008-2009 students were victims of 1.2 million non-fatal, but violent crimes (National Center for Education Statistics [IES], 2010). Current research by Renfro et al. (2003) was conducted because it was hypothesized that violence prevention programs could decrease violent behaviors in schools amongst groups that received the specific interventions.

In 1997, the Hamilton Fish Institute was formed nationally on the premise that universities could partner with schools to evaluate them and recommend research-based ideologies on the selection of appropriate violence prevention programs. As such, Eastern Kentucky (EK) and The University of Milwaukee-Wisconsin (UMW) were involved in ongoing violence prevention projects. The universities administered the National School Crime and Safety Survey (NSCSS) during similar time intervals, to similar age groups amongst a rural school and an urban school. Renfro et al. (2003) conducted a comparison study of the effectiveness of the violence prevention programs between the urban and rural school.

EK sampled a population of 610 rural students who were in 10th grade at the time of the study. UMW sampled 103 urban students in grades 9-12, the predominance of participants were in the 10th grade as well. The researchers chose these two universities data because it had the most similarities in sample data. The NSCSS included 15 scales with a multitude of questions, which were used to measure the student's perceptions and experience of school crime and violence. The initial scale was the *Motivation for Fighting* scale which consisted of 5 items asking about student's tendency to fight in response to bullying and other school related problems. The test reported a Cronbach's Alpha as a test of consistency as .79 and then the re-test reliability correlation of .66. The coefficient of internal consistency for this test was between .86 and .90, which suggests very good reliability. The following areas were scales as well: a) *Perceived Ability to Fight*, which asked students perception of their ability to win a fight; b) *Victimized by Common Aggression Scale*, which asked student to report how many times in the last 30 days they had been victims of being kicked or hit; and c) *Common Perpetration Scale*, which asked the students to indicated how many times within the last 30 days they had punched or kicked someone else. All the scales tested extremely for internal consistency ranging from .89 to .92.

The results yielded that rural students were more likely to be victims and perpetrators than their urban counterparts. The measures purported statistical significance at the respective levels of .01 and .014. The rural students self-reported that 11.3 percent, 68 out of 601 students had brought a knife to school within the last 30 days. No urban students reported having brought a knife to school within the last 30 days. Additionally, 1.5 percent of rural students reported carrying a gun to school within the past 30 days, whereas, no urban students brought a gun to school. When teacher's perceptions were asked the urban teachers stated that they did not feel safe at school, but rural teachers did, falsely indicating the perception that violence is not as much a problem in the rural community (Renfro et al., 2003). The researchers indicate that this urban school may have reported fewer problems due to increased security over the past 5 to 10 years, whereas the rural school community may really need to implement violence prevention programs.

The limitations of this study were the uneven, small sample sizes, even though there were some similarities, many differences surfaced. Additionally, the researcher's argument was overtly designed to sway the reader into believing that rural schools need violence prevention programs possibly more than urban schools, but are not receiving the same type of attention. The commonality that establishes relevancy for this current research on cyberbullying amongst adolescent urban Black females is the need to obtain students perceptions of school violence in order to establish violence prevention programs.

Much of the literature on school violence focuses on patterns of behavior and school practices as preventative measures. Additional research purports that the urban school environment has a tendency to have violent incidents occur readily, due to mirroring their surrounding neighborhoods (Vardalis & Kakar, 2000). According to Shelton, Owens, and Song (2008), urban public schools are usually placed in low-income, high-poverty, and high-crime-rate neighborhoods. Research as such prompted Watkins, Mauthner, Hewitt, Epstein, and Leonard (2005), to conduct research with the purpose of investigating whether schools differed in their approach to violence, especially in inner-city areas, where crime and violence are high.

Early research based out of London in 1967 reported findings that the school behavior problems were not directly be attributed to the neighborhood, however, more recent research suggests that difficult neighborhoods can play a significant part in the discipline problems that occur at school (Watkins & Wagner, 2000). Watkins et al. (2005) conducted their study by initially contacting 13 inner-city secondary high schools; ultimately six schools were chosen to participate in this study due to their differing approaches to dealing with school violence. Each schools pattern of school violence was obtained for a two successive school years and analyzed by calculating suspensions that were violence-related. Additionally, neighborhood violent crimes data was retrieved from the Police Performance Information Bureau. The total number of crimes was calculated one kilometer in all directions from each of the six schools. The students within this study predominately reside in the neighborhoods they attend school in.

A quantitative analysis was conducted of the suspensions and violent neighborhood crimes, additionally; qualitative interviews were conducted with staff and students, which addressed management practices of the school and connectedness of people in the school and the local community. As a result of the interviews, four themes emerged surrounding culture, communal organization, community links, and curriculum, which all affected internal and external social relationships. The qualitative data revealed that neighborhood crimes and levels of school violence did not match each other. The schools that were in the neighborhoods with the highest levels of crime did not have higher levels of suspensions. Schools in lower crime areas had similar levels of suspensions.

The findings conclude that proactive school policies and procedures, connectedness to students and community were the major factors in having low rates of suspensions. The finding precludes that conflict resulting in violence can be minimized due to the culture that is created by the schools (Watkins et al., 2005). For example, one school, which is stationed in a high crime area, taught its older students how to mentor the younger students, in attempts to prevent conflict and suspensions. This study received its crucial findings by conducting qualitative interviews, using student perceptions to inform their research practices.

Children's voices can be a tool, which if utilized properly can support the efforts to reduce violence and conflict within urban schools. Harris and Walton (2008), examined children's narrative around conflict experiences in order to provide a voice for children's lived experiences with conflict. The study took place in Memphis City Schools; the students were asked to write a story about a conflict that really happened to them. Students were given 30 minutes to author their narratives, and place them in an envelope that would be sent directly to the researchers.

The participants were fourth, fifth, and sixth graders, over 360 narratives were collected. Approximately 65 percent of the participants lived in poverty, and over half live in neighborhoods where adults surveyed state that they are afraid to walk outside. The participants were 65 percent African American and 34 percent Caucasian, less than one percent was from other ethnic minority families. The narratives averaged 115 words in length, and they were transcribed with preservation of the original punctuation and spelling. The stories primarily accounted for incidents with peers, but in some instances discussed internal conflict and conflict with adults.

There were multiple readings of the stories to develop coded categories; additionally inter-coder reliability was assessed to identify six types of conflict that occurred the most within the narratives. The coding response categories achieved .81 Kappa coefficients or above which establishes good inter-coder reliability. The six responses that occurred most frequently are (a) communication; (b) reconciliation; (c) retaliation; (d) withdrawal, (e) seeking adult help; and (f) seeking peer help. After analysis of the stories 53 percent described non-violent conflict or minor intrusions of personal space, and nine percent described life-threatening or criminal violence. Frequency coding was used to establish patterns, but the researchers found their best understanding of meaning came from the qualitative analysis of each story.

The qualitative analysis sought to understand children's narrative and social cognition related to how they talked about conflict resolution. The findings show that communication and reconciliation were the most desired responses conflict. Children indicated from their stories that communication was the consistent variable as to why many of the situations they described ended in non-violence. Approximately 95 out of 360 stories discussed ignoring and withdrawing from conflict as an option; however, one-third of the participants indicated that retaliation was the strategy they used when confronted with conflict. Adults were sought for assistance in 63 of the stories, and the typical result was isolation or punishment, only five stories indicated that the adult helped resolve the situation.

The accounts given were child's eye views of conflict that provided insight as to strategies that helped reduce and in some instances eliminate conflict. After an analysis of the data the researchers conclude that conflict should be dealt with by a head on approach, ignoring is not beneficial. Communication was the key finding that resulted in reducing and in some instances eliminating conflict. Conflict can be used to develop character and social skills (Harris & Walton, 2008).

The research denoted the potential that urban school environments have to be a dangerous place. Currently, it is unknown if cyberbullying has any implications and effects to the urban school environment, but a selective review of the literature may reveal gaps that provide a need to study its specific effects amongst urban adolescent Black females at school. The literature on the urban school environment briefly discussed different types of incidents that occur in urban schools, but heavily focused on the use of preventative pro-active strategies. A common theme within the literature was developing pro-active strategies by learning from student's perceptions and experiences. Scholarly studies such as these have recognized the importance of learning why conflict may be occurring in order to develop appropriate prevention programs, even though the National and Local governing educational bodies have not developed that same need (IES, 2010).

If cyberbullying occurs in an urban environment, it has the potential to create immense conflict. However, research does not currently inform what that may look like. Currently, it is unknown how cyberbullying can affect urban schools and adolescent Black females, but it is known that cyberbullying is a form of violence that has the potential to affect millions (Lenhart, 2006). Further review of the cyberbullying literature will provoke thought as to how it can be applied to the context of an urban school environment and Black adolescent females.

EMPIRICAL CYBERBULLYING RESEARCH

This review of the cyberbullying literature will be a very thorough review which will include many scholarly studies conducted between the years of 2000 and 2010. The cyberbullying literature will examine girl's rate of participation, lack of face-to-face conflict as a non-result, dangers associated with cyberbullying, participation and victimization, etc. Many of the studies on cyberbullying are quantitative in nature, and fail to represent why youth felt like victims or the context in which incidents occurred. The review of the literature illuminates several gaps such as an inattention to studying Blacks, specifically Black females in an urban school environment.

Due to an increase in a digitized society, cyberbullying has become more prevalent, and a need developed to study the topic approximately 11 years ago. Wollack and Mitchell (2000) conducted the first national Youth Internet Safety Survey (YISS 1). This survey focused on the exploitation of children online. The study had a sample size of approximately 1500 youth between the ages of 10 and 17. The participants were contacted by telephone between the years 1999 and 2000. The participants were asked two basic questions regarding rude or nasty comments made to someone while on the Internet, and using the Internet to embarrass someone with which they were disgruntled. Victims were identified based on their answers. It was indicated that 19 percent of the youth surveyed were involved in some sort of online aggression. When disaggregating the 19 percent, 12 percent reported being the aggressor, four percent reported being the victim, and three percent reported being both an aggressor and a victim. Youth who identified themselves as aggressive admitted to embarrassing someone online who angered them, and making rude comments to someone while they were online.

Targets of online aggression were gauged by whether or not they felt threatened or harassed and whether anyone had sent them a message or used the Internet to embarrass them within the last year. The results showed that 6 percent of the participants experienced online harassment. More than 50 percent of the participants reported that they were harassed more than once by the same individual, and 31 percent stated that they knew who their harasser was. Youth identified that 48 percent of unwanted sexual exploitation came from other youth. This finding suggested that youth who were sexually interested in one another may be participating in cyberbullying. This research may be particularly useful when applied to the context of an urban high school environment. One prediction might be that cyberbullying may be occurring more within the high school because of the familiarity and attractions students may have for each other. High Schools are a breeding ground for relational aggression (Baldry, 2004), due to forming relationships within a social space. Therefore, opportunity presents itself; now couple it with the fact that 90 percent of teens use the Internet regularly (Lenhart, 2006). Many teenage girls use the Internet for as many hours, or more than they spend at school. Research is also showing that much of the time spent online is unsupervised. Another unmentioned within this study are the implications cyberbullying can have when coupled with other circumstances, such as adverse living conditions.

Li (2005) decided to examine cyberbullying from the perspective of the urban environment; no specific recognition of race was made within the research study. This study by Li (2005) is a rare, due to its focus on the urban school environment. Li (2005) specifically focused on 177 Canadian seventh-grade students that were randomly selected. The purpose of the study was to see at what capacity cyberbullying took place among middle school aged kids in an urban environment. The results reported that traditional bullying occurred more often than cyberbullying. The survey showed 54 percent of the victims experienced traditional bullying versus 25 percent who reported being victims of cyberbullying. Out of the respondents, 33 percent said they participated in traditional bullying versus 15 percent who said they performed acts of cyberbullying.

When factored by gender, 60 percent of females reported being a victim of cyberbullying, which was 10 percent higher than males. Traditional bullying and cyberbullying were similar in the lack of incidents being reported. Individuals who participate in bullying showed a 30 percent chance that they also partake in cyberbullying. Approximately 17 percent of victims reported that they also cyberbullied other individuals. The study was very vague in reference to race, and there were no references or connotations of differentiating implications because cyberbullying occurred in an urban environment.

The following year, Li (2006) surveyed 264 middle school students to examine gender differences on reporting incidents of cyberbullying to adults. Three urban districts were randomly surveyed. The results were similar to 2005 with 25 percent of the students admitted to being victims of cyberbullying. Victims reported traditional bullying four percent less than the previous year. In 2006, the students admitted that 50 percent of them knew someone who had been cyberbullied. A small percentage of students admitted to cyberbullying others. The survey also concluded that males were more likely to cyberbully than females. This is not supported by other research on this topic (Lenhart, 2006). A limitation of this study is the small sample size; this may be why the findings do not equate to results in other studies. This study also concluded that students weren't likely to tell adults about cyberbullying when it occurred, generally because they felt the adult would not do anything about it. The aforementioned results are consistent with other bodies of literature (National i-SAFE Survey, 2004). This implication presents a need to understand how and when cyberbullying is occurring in the urban environment.

Another national study which had a bigger sample size supports that parents are not as aware as they think they are regarding their child's Internet usage. In 2005, i-SAFE conducted a survey for a second time, this time using a sample size of 12,000 students ranging from fifth to twelfth grade. The results stated that 22 percent of the students knew someone who was a victim of cyberbullying, and 19 percent admitted to saying hurtful things to others online. The i-SAFE surveys exposed a huge gap between parents and their children. Ninety-three percent of parents stated that they gave their children rules to follow online, whereas, 37 percent of children said that their parents gave them rules online. Ninety-five percent of the parents also felt that they knew a lot about their children's Internet activities while 41 percent of the children stated that they shared information with their parents.

Parents are presuming to really know what their children are doing online. This survey speaks to the need to establish better parental supervision. According to Berson et al. (2002), many teens reported to being online between six to nine hours a day and 60 percent reported giving out personal information over the

Internet. Li, (2005), reported that 25 percent of their participants had been cyberbullied. The research implies that cyberbullying and other Internet crimes are being committed on a regular basis; it may behoove parents to better monitor their children's online activities.

This current study examined aggressive behavior among youth online. Ybarra and Mitchell (2004a) used the data from the first Youth Internet Safety Survey (YISS 1) to guide their original research study. The researchers conducted a cross-sectional nationally-representative telephone survey. The study focused heavily on parent-child relationships and psychosocial attributes of the aggressors. Youth were interviewed, along with one parent or guardian. Forty-four percent of cyberbullies, who harassed, reported having a negative emotional bond with their caregiver. Nineteen percent of individuals who did not partake in harassment reported that they had destitute emotional bonds with their caregiver. Substance abuse played a part in whether harassment occurred online. Thirty-two percent of the respondents admitted to substance abuse while only 10 percent of the non-harassers reported involvement in substance abuse.

Additionally, online harassment occurred more to victims of traditional face to face bullying. The survey indicated that 51 percent of respondents, who harass, versus 30 percent of non-harassers, were victims of traditional bullying. Twenty percent of the respondents reported also being victims of cyber harassment, versus only four percent of non-harassers. The analysis of the survey revealed that bullies and cyberbullies alike have poor connections with caregivers and in return it may cause poor psychosocial relationships that may create a more likely chance that harassment will occur.

This study does not take into account for adverse living conditions. It is said Black urban youth may respond differently to an aggressive situation due to consistent exposure to adverse living conditions. Herrenkohl et al. (2001), warn that Black youth are exposed to violence in their communities, offered inadequate support, denied reasonable opportunities, and, as such, are more likely to respond violently in adverse situations. Approximately 70 percent of urban Black youth live in neighborhoods associated with poverty and violence (USDHHS, 2001). Cyberbullying has the potential to manifest itself in a manner within an urban environment that could lend itself to physical violence, but without further research, it is an unknown implication.

The results of the aforementioned studies are continuous with the results from the first i-Safe study. This study presents a reality of exactly how hurtful information is passed online between youthful cyberbullying offenders. I-SAFE America, Inc. (2004), a not-for-profit agency whose mission is to "educate and empower youth to safely and responsibly take control of their Internet experiences" (National i-SAFE Survey, 2004, p. 3), conducted a national study completed by 1,566 participants who ranged from fourth to eighth grade. There was a pre- and post-assessment given. The pre-assessment was given before the i-SAFE curriculum was taught. The i-SAFE survey was composed of quantitative and qualitative questions that asked for information such as the amount of time spent on the Internet. The post assessment was taken immediately upon the completion of the course. An additional assessment was given three to six weeks later, as well. Among the participants, 57 percent said that someone had said hurtful things to them online while 53 percent admitted to saying hurtful things to others. The respondents reported that 42 percent had been bullied online, and seven percent said that it happened frequently. When discussing threats, 35 percent reported that they occurred, and 20 percent stated that threats happened via email. Some researchers have formulated a well-calculated opinion that cyber bullying occurs more frequently amongst females (Berson, Berson, & Ferron, 2002).

Adolescence can be challenging for females and is compounded when the potential for victimization through cyberbullying is introduced into the equation. When adolescent girls participate in relational aggressive tactics, it is a form of fighting without physically hitting anyone. Berson, Berson, and Ferron (2002) conducted an online survey to assess risky behaviors of girls. The survey size was 10,800 girls who ranged from 12 to 18 years of age. The survey was broken up into three areas, online routines, patterns of online usage, and supervised activities online. There was a total of 19 multiple choice questions. Over 90 percent of the girls reported that their computer was in an isolated access area. A quarter of the surveyed population stated that they were online six to nine hours a day and 12 percent stated they were online 10-12 hours a day.

During this time period, only half of the girls surveyed reported that they were supervised occasionally. Occasionally, in this instance, is defined as being checked on from time to time. Most of the time online was spent instant messaging or emailing with friends. Respondents reported that parents and teachers discussed online safety. It was reported that parents discussed online safety about 70 percent of the time, whereas teachers did 35 percent of the time. Personal information was given out by 60 percent of the teens. This survey was conducted before the popularity of social networking exploded. At second glance, most of the time was spent emailing and instant messaging with friends. Currently, individuals can connect with multiple friends at a time due to social networking (Hinduja & Patchin, 2008). This is an important factor because social networking allows people to connect, establish relationships, and communicate with the masses. Girls, specifically, express an innate need to establish connections with others socially (Brown & Gilligan, 1992). The desire to fulfill this need often leads girls to become victims of emotional attack. Feeling vulnerable often causes girls to overcompensate by guarding themselves at all times. Berson et al. (2002) report that three percent of the teens admitted to originating threatening comments, and 15 percent reported to having "disturbing conversation" online, therefore lending proof to the fact that relational aggression is occurring online.

This study measured dangerous behavior associated with online activity among females. The findings represent a large portion of girls who are engaging in dangerous behavior while in cyberspace. The identifiable gap within this study is represented by only 35 percent of teachers who chose to educate their students on cybersafety. It was important to note that Berson et al. (2002), state that the more girls are online, the greater the chance may be that violent behavior may occur. A limitation of this study is the anonymity in which the data was collected via the Internet. This may be problematic due to the possibility that the girls could adulterate their personal data.

This survey is important due to its large survey size of girls and their online behaviors. It gave insight into the types of behaviors occurring. This research is useful when discussing girls in general, but it does not lend specific information to Black adolescent girls in an urban high school. Additional research committed specifically to Black females may be useful. The research shows that cyberbullying is a problem and the specific implications it may have amongst the populations that have been studied. Additional research supports the prevalence of cyberbullying amongst females.

Research often states that the Internet creates a genderized role reversal with traditional bullying, which occurs more frequently amongst males (Espelage, Holt, & Henkel, 2003). Kowalski and Limber (2007), conducted a survey among 3,767 middle school children in grades six to eight. Their survey collected data on traditional bullying and cyberbullying. The information that was collected for the survey was based on the previous two months. A total of six elementary and middle schools were surveyed across the southern and eastern regions of the United Sates. Eleven percent of the sample reported being bullied, and seven percent reported being victims of cyberbullying or participating in it.

In a two month period, four percent said they committed an act of bullying at least once. 25 percent of the girls versus 11 percent of boys indicated being victims of cyberbullying. In contrast, 13 percent of the females versus eight percent of the males admitted to cyberbullying others. The examination of traditional bullying showed differing results across gender: a little over 14 percent of the boys surveyed, versus 13 percent of the girls, disclosed they had participated in traditional face to face bullying. In a two month period, eight percent of boys and five percent of girls disclosed that they had participated in traditional face to face bullying at least two to three times. Conversely, the study also showed that some cyberbullies may not bully at school, but the traditional school bully may become a target online. Cyberbullying can have many implications.

This study was designed to assess how cyberbullying is affecting youth. Patchin and Hinduja (2006) examined the magnitude and implications of cyberbullying on youth. Unique methods were used to collect data; a link was placed on a website of a music group whose popularity was in line with the pinpointed age group. Consent to participate in Internet studies can be an issue, but the researchers did an informed consent by adding a checkbox and submit button if the users agreed to participate. Four components of the surveys framework were: (a) demographic data was solicited early on in the study, due to research showing it may decrease rates of attrition; (b) participants of the survey were able to complete the survey on one screen; (c) participants were entered into a random drawing with the possibility of winning autographed photos of the band; and, (d) surveys that had responses that were all the same were thrown out.

The total number of respondents was 571, with 384 individuals who were under the age of 18. The majority of the respondents were Caucasian females though the music that the band played that night may have contributed to the environment's limited population. The researchers of this study indicated that there may be a technological divide between some populations, indicating that some are not "privy" to access. Most of the participant age ranged from 12 years old to 20 years old. More than half of the participants spoke English and were from the United States. Online bullying was clearly defined by threats, hurtful names, continuous abrupt teasing, and sexual harassment. The results of the survey indicated that 11 percent reported bullying, 29 percent reported being a victim, and 47 percent stated that they were a witness to cyberbullying that occurred.

Cyberbullying occurred most frequently in chat rooms. Cyberbullying experiences were then related to traditional experiences of bullying. Other important results addressed behaviors that were associated with bullying. Sixty percent of respondents reported being ignored, 50 percent reported being disrespected by others, 21.4 percent threatened by others, 30 percent called names, 20 percent picked on, 19 percent made fun of, and 18.8 percent stated they had rumors spread about them. The average youth reported that they had been bullied in a chat room approximately 3.36 times within a month's time. In one instance, a respondent reported that he had been bullied in a chat room 50 times within 30 days. Email and text messaging were also a prime source for cyberbullying to occur. Close to one-third of the respondents stated that they were affected at school by cyberbullying, and fewer than nine percent of respondents said they would tell a grownup. Thus, a conclusion can be made, stating that youth are affected at school by cyberbullying, but adults are not privy to the information, which leads to implications that produce a need to study specifically how youth are affected at school. This specific study will do so from the perspective of urban Black adolescent females.

This study by Patchin and Hinduja (2006) had several limitations. The first limitation is the narrow representation of different ethnicities based on certain selections of popular music. There were only four Black people represented in the entire survey. It was discussed that the sample in the survey may not mirror the real world. Another problem that could have occurred is a misrepresentation of the participant's ages. There was no way to determine if the respondents were telling the truth about how old they were. This research should be looked at carefully and cautiously due to the poor representation of the minority groups. A larger sample size may help to counteract this problem. A study that examined the effects of cyberbullying among Black girls in an urban high school could be unique to the body of research on cyberbullying. The study also suggests a need to examine further whether or not cyberbullying threats are later turned into actual physicality among school-aged children.

To begin to understand how cyberbullying affects the school environment, a correlation should be made with traditional bullying. Li, 2005; Li, 2006, state that there is no disconnect between cyberbullying and traditional bullying. A continuation of that thought and a further examination was done by Ybarra, Diener-

West, and Leaf (2007). 1588 youth were participants in this cross-sectional survey. The main foci of this study were to examine the overlap between cyberbullying and traditional bullying and to establish any correlations with school discipline problems and cyberbullying. This longitudinal study required that each adult in the household be extremely knowledgeable about their child's Internet usage.

The main measures included Internet harassment and school functioning. Some of the factors examined were rude or nasty comments, spreading of rumors, and aggressive, threatening comments, academic performance, skipping school, detentions, suspensions, and carrying a weapon to school within the last 30 days. Results from this study showed that 64 percent of the youth surveyed reported that they were harassed online, but that they were not bullied at school. In this study approximately 35 percent reported being a victim of cyberbullying, and 8 percent reported being a victim more than once in a month. Almost 18 percent of the population said that they experienced frequent harassment overlapping on and offline. Nearly half the youth who reported abuse online and at school reported distress from the Internet incident.

There was a strong connection between youth who were harassed online and skipping school, being suspended, having detention, and carrying a weapon to school. It was revealed that youth who were victims of cyberbullying were eight times more likely to carry a weapon to school with them. Threats and rumors online caused about 24 percent of youth to carry a weapon to school. Skipping school developed as the most prevalent effect of being bullied online. Current statistics purport that in 2008, approximately 78 percent of the violent crimes registered happened in urban schools (School Violence, Weapons, Crime, and Bullying, 2010). This is an alarming statistic that speaks to a need for preventative measures. Currently, it is unknown how cyberbullying specifically affects students in an urban environment, but if data reports that online bullying specifically leads to an eight times greater chance that a student brings a gun to school it may be an indication of a need to study it further.

Overlap was not found to be significant between cyberbullying and traditional bullying, but a strong correlation was made between Internet harassment and school discipline problems. An additional note is that youth who were victimized online frequently reported having psychosocial problems. It was also established that they had poor parental monitoring and low emotional bonds with their caregiver. A limitation of this study is that the findings were exclusive to a traditional school setting; homeschool was not considered. This study has implications that school related problems do carry over from cyberbullying. About 12 percent of the participants were Black, and about 10 percent of those respondents reported that they were frequently harassed online. That shows a major significance that isn't being discussed in the literature; that cyberbullying is occurring with Black youth and may severely affect school discipline problems.

In a study conducted by Raskauskas and Stolz (2007), a connection between cyberbullying and traditional bullying discussed implications for high school aged children. The study was composed of 84, 13-18-year-olds. The youth participated in a questionnaire about their participation in cyberbullying and traditional bullying. The major results of the study showed that cell phone text messaging was the most frequent form of bullying. The results showed that 48 percent of the victims experienced cyberbullying via text messaging. The most common form of traditional bullying was physical. Forty-five percent of traditional bullying victims experience being physically bullied. Additionally, it was reported that 93 percent of the youth were affected negatively due to cyberbullying. This study was able to show a 48 percent overlap between cyberbullying and traditional bullying. The results also concluded that 85 percent of the victims were victimized by traditional and cyberbullying. An overwhelming 94 percent of the bullies participated in traditional and cyberbullying.

This study made a strong correlation between cyberbullying and traditional bullying Raskauskas and Stolz (2007) did not specifically look at schools in this study, but it was implied that although cyberbullying happened at home, it may be related to what is occurring at school. To make the correlation, a Chi-square analysis was conducted. The number (n=35) of traditional victims involved in cyberbullying was higher than (n=25) those not involved in cyberbullying. Results showed that only one traditional bully did not engage in cyberbullying. Ybarra and Mitchell (2004a) state that cyberbullying may even be more damaging than traditional bullying because students can be victims in their own homes. It was also indicated that cyberbullying should not be treated any differently than traditional bullying when dealt with by school officials. The data in this study was disaggregated by ethnicity, but it was not reported on or displayed in the findings. The study's sample size was small, but it showed a strong overlap between cyberbullying and traditional bullying. This information may be important for schools to examine, and possibly develop intervention strategies to assist with curbing this potential problem.

Typically, research indicates that online conflict does not create offline consequences, but current research argues differently. Patchin and Hinduja (2007) address online antics that create offline consequences. The General Strain Theory was found to be connected to cyberbullying; a correlation from the data was made to strengthen Patchin and Hinduja's argument and add theoretical value. In a snapshot, the General Strain Theory states that when people commit crimes or exploit others, it usually has to do with other stresses in their lives. The data connected cyberbullying as a strain that may directly affect an individual's school performance. Cyberbullying may be the catalyst that produces negative emotions, and the victims may channel their strained emotions to retaliate offline on the initial aggressor. The researchers indicated that negative fears associated with cyberbullying might cause psychological damage to the victim. It was noted that cyberbullying may cause individuals much strain and lead to school avoidance.

Additionally, Patchin and Hinduja conducted a survey in 2004-2005 with a sample of 1,388 adolescents who go online. The initial survey encompassed 6,800 participants, but an overwhelming response was provided by girls. Girls accounted for 82 percent of the survey. The researchers felt there might have been bias in the data, so they chose a random group of females to proportionate the data. The results of the survey indicated that 36 percent of girls and 32 percent of boys were victims of cyberbullying. Cyberbullying occurred most frequently in chat rooms, and through online text messaging. Interestingly enough, 35 percent of victims reported that cyberbullying did not affect them. In contrast, 34 percent stated they felt frustrated and over 30 percent said it made them angry. Correlated results indicated that a strain was caused by cyberbullying and that it may severely impact school violence and truancy. Truancy from school may need to be examined further when placed in the context of urban high schools and black females. The researchers noted that older youth may be more inclined to tell an adult or someone else altogether.

The implications of this study suggest that cyberbullying and school violence connect, but it does not directly place it in an urban context, nor it is it viewed through the lens of Black females. This research indicated that 82 percent of females responded to the survey. Some bias may have occurred, but even as the sample was randomized, more females reported that they had been a victim of cyberbullying than males, which was concurrent with Patchin and Hinduja's (2006) research, as well. The implications are that girls are heavily affected by cyberbullying, but the research thus far has been limited, and there has been no representation of Black females in an urban context. The original research to be conducted will focus on urban Black adolescent females who are at least 18 years of age and the effects cyberbullying had on them and their high school experience. According to Patchin and Hinduja (2007), they will be more inclined to report on the incidences.

To further understand how cyberbullying occurs among younger populations composed of pre-teens (6-11), a survey was conducted by an Opinion Research Corporation. This study specifically reported on how Black youth engaged in Internet usage. Until this study was conducted, the research has focused mostly on youth between the ages of 12 to17, not specifically disaggregating for race. In this study conducted by Caravan (2006), it was revealed that 17 percent of 503 preteens had been victims of cyberbullying. The study used a random digit dial to sample the various households and varied from many other studies because the data was also disaggregated by race.

The results were not analyzed with race specifically in mind, but that category was used to help the researchers get a clearer picture of preteens that experience cyberbullying. It was discovered that four percent of the youth had been victims of cyberbullying more frequently than four times in one year. Conversely, 79 percent said they did not have any form of cyberbullying committed against them. Thirty-seven percent of the youth reported that they were victims of some sort of cyberbullying. The most common form reported was being teased about their appearance. When the different forms of cyberbullying were disaggregated, 23 percent said they were victimized by email, 18 percent in chat rooms, 12 percent from instant messages, and seven percent from text.

When reviewing the information and looking at the Black population of respondents, 38 percent reported using the Internet for more than an hour a day, and 36 percent reported less than an hour of usage time, thus showing that 74 percent of the Black youth surveyed had access to a computer and the Internet. A continuation of the data review showed 44 percent of Black youth used a cell phone during the day. Eighteen percent reported being a victim of cyberbullying, and three percent indicated that they had been a victim of cyberbullying more than five times in a year. The most prevalent form of cyberbullying when disaggregated by race was concurrent with the total population, in which making fun of one's appearance topped the list. Black youth reported that 23 percent of cyberbullying occurred due to email, 23 percent from comments on a website, 23 percent from an instant message, 12 percent from an embarrassing photo, and 23 percent from a text message. When Black youth were asked where they may have gotten the messages, 32 percent said from home, 45 percent from school, and 44 percent from a friend's house. When asked if they knew their bully, 67 percent stated that they did know them.

The data presented is important because it provided a snapshot of how Black youth use the Internet and how they may be victimized online as well. The limitations to that specific portion of the data are that Black youth represented a very small sample size. It may be too small to be considered significant. This study did not specifically examine the race of the individuals who initiated the bullying online. In this study, 74 percent of the Black youth surveyed went online regularly. This is huge because research says that Black youth may not have access to technology and that cyberbullying occurs more in affluent suburbs. Epstein and Kazmierczack (2007) suggest that cyberbullying was a behavior that was observed more commonly in affluent suburbs and affecting girls more than boys. That does not say that black youth cannot live in affluent neighborhoods, but many do not. However, the Pew Research Center (2010) conducted a national study that purported African Americans lead the way in the use of cell phone data applications. Additionally, Blacks and other minorities are more likely to use a cell phone than Caucasians. Sixty-four percent of Black Americans are wi-fi users. It was duly noted that Blacks have a tendency to take advantage of the data features offered on their mobile phones at a rate nearly four percent higher than Caucasians. This indicates that blacks are connecting online through their mobile phones, removing a once thought of idea referred to as the digital divide.

The significance of studying urban Black adolescent females is because the literature has proclaimed that cyberbullying may manifest itself more aggressively amongst urban Black females (Herrenkohl et al., 2001). One of the most common uses of the Internet is social networking, a virtual space in which bullying can readily occur (Hinduja & Patchin, 2008). Social networking is a popular pastime that increases access to one's peers which, when coupled with a lack of online supervision, facilitates cyberbullying readily. Currently, it is unknown how Black females participate in this form of cyberbullying and how it affects them. A review of the literature on social networking will explain the platform where frequent cyberbullying occurs.

SOCIAL NETWORKING

This literature review will address how social networking is a huge part of the DYC that very often removes the anonymity of the Internet and makes individuals aware of their friends and harassers, which in turn can impact the school environment because students have the ability form relationships or to confront their advisories. An additional characteristic of social networking is that it can assist in spreading information at the speed of light, whether it is helpful or damaging (Hinduja & Patchin, 2008). These illuminations and others will reveal a need to further understand how Black adolescent females partake in social networking due to a lack of discourse provided by the literature.

Individuals who partake in social networking usually do so for various reasons. Social networking can support positive and negative motivations. While some seek to connect or reconnect with friends in spite of vast distances, others use social networking sites to propagate rumors heard in social settings such as school. According to Surra and Milardo (1991), social networking opens up opportunities for interplay among people who have similar past, and present experiences, and relationships. It was reported in 2007 that over 150 million people are registered users of MySpace, one of the most popular social networking sites (Lenhart, Madden, Macgill, & Smith, 2007).

The fear that the researchers express with social networking revolves around sexual predators and pedophiles that prey on adolescents who post identifiable information on public personal profile pages. Hinduja and Patchin (2008) conducted this quantitative study due to the demonization of MySpace because of irresponsible usage of technology and the need to ascertain the information that youth are posting. An extensive content analysis of randomly sampled MySpace profile pages (1,475) showed that youth are publicly including a picture on their page 57 percent of the time, listing their school 28 percent, which revealed their full name 8.8 percent, and 0.3 percent are even posting their telephone numbers. The results show that youth may be using the Internet more responsibly than the researchers originally thought, but Internet safety issues are still occurring. Hinduja and Patchin (2008) recommend that adults can help reduce online victimization by supervising online usage, by promoting online safety and ethical use of computers, investigate any potential dangerous incidents.

Previously cyberbullying was considered to be an anonymous crime, and the dangers were hard to report because no one knew who was committing the offense. Research conducted within the last few years' reports that almost half of the online users know the person who is committing the cyber harassment (Wollack, Mitchell, & Finkelhor, 2006). This may be due to social networking sights. Social networking affords individuals the opportunity to view each other's personal information. Wollack, Mitchell, and Finkelhor (2006) conducted a second Youth Internet Safety Study (YISS 2) out of the University of New Hampshire. The YISS 2 was conducted nationally by telephone; there were 1500 randomly chosen participants ranging in age from 10 to 17. The focus of the study was to examine how youth are victimized online, and other associated factors.

The survey results were similar to the previous year's study and stated that nine percent of Internet users had been harassed, and 32 percent had been harassed more than three times. Fifty-eight percent of the identified individuals committing harassment were youth, 50 percent male, and 28 percent female. Results showed that 38 percent of the youth surveyed experienced being distressed from negative cyber interactions. The four areas that caused the most distress were: (a) if the online users were preadolescents, (b) whether or not offline aggression occurred because of online interaction (e.g., physical altercation, phone call), (c) if pictures were asked for, and (d) if adults targeted the youth. Results revealed that chat rooms are not as likely to cause youth distress. The YISS 2 also indicated an increase in cyberbullying from 2000-2005. The implications that online aggression may sometimes be followed by offline line aggression may be significant when put in the context of Black girls and urban high schools. Statistics on urban violence have purported that 38 percent of urban school violence occurs due to Black youth (National Center for Education Statistics [IES], 2010). Additionally, Ybarra, Diener-West, and Leaf, (2007) report that being harassed online significantly increases the possibility of students carrying weapons to school. Knowing the potential of cyberbullying and that frequent violence occurs among urban adolescent Black youth, are reasons to inquire further how cyberbullying that occurs on social networking sites has the potential to affect the urban school environment. If relational aggression turns into physical altercations while youth are at school, it could create an unsafe environment. This study did not delve deep into the effect that social networking has when acts of relational aggression have occurred, but it did provide implications that offline aggression could occur due to online conflict that may often occur due to social networking.

Further research on the ways that cyberbullying is most prevalent may shed light into how it is affecting adolescent girls in school. Lenhart (2007) did a study through the PEW Internet and American Life project containing a total of 935 adolescent participants. This study used a mixed methodology of surveys and focus groups. The surveys were conducted on the phone with participants whose ages ranged from 12 to 17. Seven focus groups were conducted in two different areas within the United States; one group was held online. The online group consisted of high school aged boys and girls, whereas the other groups were single gendered. Youth in grades seven through 12 participated in the other focus groups.

The results of the study indicate that almost 70 percent of teens said that offline bullying occurred more than online bullying. In contrast, 30 percent of youth felt cyberbullying was more prevalent. When the data was disaggregated by gender, it was reported that 38 percent of girls experienced being victims of cyberbullying, compared to 26 percent of boys. Out of the girls surveyed, 41 percent between the ages 15-17 announced that they were victims of cyberbullying, showing that it was more prevalent in older teenage girls. Teenagers who use social networking sites reported almost an 18 percent higher chance of being a victim of cyberbullying. Could youth feel that they are being victimized by bullying more due to the ease and regularity that relationships are formed on social networking sites? While some seek to connect or reconnect with friends in spite of vast distances, others use social networking sites to propagate rumors heard in social settings such as school. When rumors start in a school building, the social networking site provides an outlet for rumors to grow and spread vastly at speeds that could not be done without Internet access (Hinduja & Patchin, 2008).

This particular research was very quantitative in nature and did not explore how social networking affected the school environment. However, it did report that a total of 32 percent of teens were a victim of cyberbullying. The data showed that 15 percent of text, IM, and private emails got forwarded to someone else, and/or posted in a public place online. It was also reported that 13 percent of the teens spread rumors online; while 13 percent received threatening messages from via text, email, or IM. Six percent of the respondents reported that a picture was sent of them, without their permission. In all instances, a form of relational aggression was used to manipulate or hurt someone else. Additional literature review on relational aggression will provide a greater understand on how it manifests itself through cyberbullying.

RELATIONAL AGGRESSION

This section of the literature review will focus on relational aggression, but it will bridge cyberbullying, urban school violence, and relational aggression literature by discussing how cyberbullying a form of relational aggression has the ability to create conflict within the school environment. When cyberbullying, a form of relational aggression, categorized as disrespect online, occurs among urban Black youth. Currently, there is no research reporting how it manifests itself in social contexts. Relational aggression has the potential to manifest itself in anywhere that there is a social setting. Previously relational aggression was limited to public places such as school, but now due to the Digital Youth Culture (DYC), relational aggression is additionally situated in cyberspace amongst social networking. DYC places a high value on social networking, IM, and texting (McQuade et al., 2009). To further understand relational aggression a concise empirical review of literature that explains relational aggression will assist readers to further understand how it applies to cyberbullying.

Relational aggression is an overarching term that is the umbrella for different forms of aggression that do not include physical violence. A study conducted by Xie, Farmer, and Cairns 2003, examine forms of aggression, by conducting semi-structured individual interviews. Often aggression involves a physical and/or verbal exchange, but this study also examines more disguised, manipulative aggression geared toward affecting one's social status and relationships. First, different forms of aggression were identified: (a) social aggression and indirect aggression refer to acts that are non-confrontational, such as gossiping and social alienation, talking about someone behind their backs, telling secrets and betraying trust, (b) direct relational aggression includes actions between individuals, including deliberate ignoring, threatening to refrain from one's friendship, and alienation from group activities, (c) physical aggression refers to any act where an infliction of damage occurs from physical force, and (d) verbal aggression refers to the use of damaging words attempting to hurt or humiliate another person. It was reported by the authors that African American boys and girls have higher levels of physical aggression compared to other ethnic groups.

In this particular study, 489 participants from four inner-city high schools were involved. One-third of the families in the area studied were below the poverty level. The participation rate for this study was 60 percent. The participants in this study were specifically asked to identify both same- and opposite-sex peers that bothered or caused them trouble and describe the conflicts thoroughly. Mixed methods were used. Some of the qualitative codes were (a) identifying other persons involved in conflict, (b) the structure of the conflict, and (c) the participants' aggressive behavior. Xie et al. used an Interpersonal Competence Scale that was filled out for each participant by a teacher or a counselor. Conflict was used as the central unit of analysis. Over half of the conflicts involved physical aggression, one-third verbal aggression, and authorities intervened in both cases. Direct relational aggression was more likely to occur in girls than boys, but physical aggression occurred more in boys. Verbal aggression yielded no significant difference between boys and girls, only amongst different grade levels. Girls in grade seven were reported to have higher levels of verbal aggression. The p value was < .05. Verbal aggression across grade levels only achieved a statistical value of p<.001.

Traditional bullying is deeply rooted with relational aggression. Empirically, Nansel et al., (2001) measured the self-reported outcomes of bullying among 15, 686 participants in grades six through 10 in public and private schools nationally. It was found that 30 percent of the sample reported some sort of involvement in bullying, either as victim or perpetrator. The study was part of a larger international study. In some countries, up to 70 percent of the individuals surveyed reported that they had experienced being bullied at least once. It was also found that boys have a tendency to physically bully or be bullied more than girls. Females reported that when they were bullied, it usually involved sexual comments or rumors. Bullying occurred more frequently in grades six through eight. The findings show that there were patterns among the bullies that indicated psychosocial adjustment issues. The study's limitation was a broad focus that did a cross-sectional analysis of the data but did not account for the direction of the relationships among the variables. Looking at aggressive behaviors, but specifically relationally aggressive behaviors among school-aged children that reflect the population of this study can create a sense as to how it can mitigate into a school environment.

Aggressive behaviors among middle school students were contextualized by examining peer groups in a longitudinal study conducted by Espelage et al., (2003). Espelage et al. conducted a short-term, longitudinal study in a mid-western town. The study was conducted in two waves; the initial wave was in 1999, and the next wave was in 2000. The target sample for the initial wave was the entire student body composed of 475 students. Parental permission slips were sent home under the auspice that they are returned only if the parents did not want their child to participate. Out of 475 students, 422 students were able to participate, equaling

93 percent possible participation rate. The participants were composed of 51 percent females and 49 percent males. When disaggregating the data by grade, 30 percent of the participants were in sixth grade, 33 percent seventh grade, and 38 percent were in eighth grade. Out of the 422 students able to participate in Wave one, 384 (91 percent) successfully completed the survey. Wave two was not as successful, with 38 participants from Wave one choosing not to partake in Wave two for various reasons. The subject pool was over 90 percent Caucasian students. A comparison was done between Wave one and Wave two for sex, age, grade, bullying and a fighting scale score. The p-value was less than .05 in all cases except for bullying. Statistical value was shown due to the fact that students who participated in both waves of data had significantly higher Wave 1 bullying scores (M=1.72, SD=.69). When analyzed further a small effect size of .01 showed limited significance.

The study was conducted during students' free periods. The survey was generally given to approximately seven to 15 students at a time. The students were told that they were going to be asked questions about their friends, feelings, and aggression. The survey consisted of three sections: demographics, bullying and fighting scales, and peer nomination tasks. Bullying was measured by a nine-item Illinois Bullying Scale, which examined the scale of teasing, name calling, rumors and social exclusion. The questions focused on a span of the last 30 days and if/how they teased, upset, and excluded others from their group. Fighting was analyzed by using the five-item Illinois Fight Scale. It was also representative of a 30-day span. It included questions on physical altercations, threatening to hit, hitting first or hitting back, and fighting students they perceived they could easily beat. The data from both the Wave one bullying and fight scales showed a Cronbach alpha coefficient of .87. Students were asked to list the names of students who bullied others and those with whom they hung out the most.

The results indicated that males reported more bullying than females $p<.001$ and sixth graders reported less bullying than seventh or eighth graders. Sixth and eighth graders reported less fighting than seventh graders (n^2 =.02). Only seven percent of the girls versus 22 percent of the boys were placed in the bullying group. There was no significant trend across grades of students classified as bullies representing a p-value < .05. The self-reported data showed that males were more likely to be nominated as bullies than females ($p<.001$, n^2 =.05). Many students did not identify bullies in the peer-nominated section, which produced a lot of zero variables. This resulted in bully and fight scale data needing to be used. The results showed a significant difference between bullies and non-bullies. The bully group which was self-reported showed a standard deviation (SD= 6.45) bully nominations, whereas the self-reported non-bully group received a standard deviation (SD= 1.10) nominations. Results did not differ much in Wave two. Wave one was also used to predict aggression within one's primary peer group at Wave two. When focusing on 138 seventh graders, it yielded 20 cliques ranging from 3 to 12 members each. The cliques were predominately sex-specific, except for one.

The mixed-sex group was composed of five males and one female. Therefore, the data was calculated with the males. Initially the researchers thought that grade would be a factor in predicting aggression among peer groups, but it was not. Results also purported that peer group bullying influenced bullying levels within each peer group at wave 2 (t=6.25, p<.001). Overall, the research suggests that individuals embrace other individuals who have similar frequencies with bullying and fighting. The researchers indicate that reciprocal socialization occurs from frequent interaction. It was found through the longitudinal design, controlling for gender, that peer groups are predictive of behavior over time. Bullying may lead to more serious forms of aggression later in life. This study has value because it represents the influence that peer groups could potentially have on bullying during middle school. Additionally, the researchers reported that peers, not the victim or the bully, were involved in 85 percent of occurrences with bullying.

A limitation of this study was that peer-group process variables were not examined. Another limitation is that the students' peer groups were limited to only eight nominations, which may not be completely representative of all their friends. This study did not look at level three variables such as school climate, anti-bullying, or cyberbullying. The influence of this study may be useful in future research that involves how peer groups affect each other in regards to aggression. The use of cyberbullying as a factor could possibly change some of the outcomes.

Another research study that focused on the victimization of adolescent girls through relationally aggressive tactics was conducted by Burgess-Proctor, Patchin, and Hinduja (2009). A mixed method approach was used by the researchers. When the data was analyzed, it was shown that some qualitative and quantitative responses overlapped. Victimization was an area that overlapped within methodologies. Girls often described being called fat or ugly; similar frequency occurred around gossip and rumors being spread. The study sample size was 3,141 girls between the ages eight and 17; the mean age was 13 to 17. Almost 70 percent of the respondents were in high school in grades nine to 12. The most important factor may be that 78 percent of the respondents were Caucasian/white females, additional proof that further research may need to be done with a concentration on urban black females. The researchers of this study commented that the population they studied was "disproportionately" white.

The survey asked open-ended questions. The questions were presented in this manner so girls could further explain their experiences with cyberbullying. The study results revealed that 38 percent of the girls had been victims of cyberbullying within their lifetimes. Disaggregated further, 11 percent announced they had been threatened, 43 percent announced being disrespected, and 46 percent stated they had been ignored. The most prevalent source of cyberbullying for the girls was unwanted sexual advances. It was noted that the sexual advances often came from an anonymous source. Some researchers report that anonymity is a major contributor to online aggression and cyberbullying. Aggression is occurring, and it is occurring online due to anonymity and comfort of use (Lisante, 2005). This currents study did an analysis of how frequently the girls knew their online bully. A total of 1,203 girls reported they were victims of cyberbullying. Most of those girls reported that they knew the bully from school, that the bully was a friend 31 percent of the time, and someone else from school 36.4 percent of the time. The qualitative data showed cyberbullying quite frequently came from the girls' ex-boyfriends. When victimization occurred by a stranger, it was usually from someone with an unrecognizable screen name.

The findings of the quantitative and qualitative data overlapped. In both cases, rumors being spread online were most common, exemplifying relational aggressive tactics. The quantitative data showed that 55 percent of the youth felt that cyberbullying had no negative effect on them. In contrast, 27 percent indicated it affected them at home, and 22 percent stated it affected them at school. This type of study can help one understand the implications that cyberbullying may have on female victims. The respondents to this survey were overwhelmingly Caucasian females. This study did not examine how race affected cyberbullying, or if it did at all. The research from every study in this literature review has neglected the fact that urban Black girls in high school may be a part of cyberbullying, also.

Urban black adolescent females and relational aggression. Some urban Black females may not conform to society's perception of how and when relational aggression should end. When cyberbullying a form of relational aggression, categorized as disrespect online, occurs among urban Black youth. Currently, there is no research reporting how it manifests itself in social contexts. A current theme amongst the literature is the notion that respect is of the utmost importance to urban Black females and fighting for it. Many urban Black youth have an ingrained value of respect that becomes a microsystem of their socialization (Deutsch & Jones, 2008). The "Code of the Streets" as defined by Anderson (1999) is a set of informal rules dependent on a search for respect that governs public social relations among inner-city residents. Respect for some is more important than money. Research literature will indicate how relational aggression has the potential to create conflict among Black adolescent females.

In a qualitative study conducted by Jones (2004), a subject was interviewed and made reference to a fight that all stemmed because an individual (a Black Female) was disrespected. The fight was initiated by a comment from one girl to another about her sneakers being ugly. A few comments went back and forth, and then a fight ensued. A comment later made by the interviewee was that she expects to have to fight in school. This type of attitude may be further explained through Jones's work by her surveillance theory. Jones' use of surveillance is described as a constant monitoring whether be it by security, boys viewing the Black girls curves, or other girls gazing making relationally aggressive comments to their peers (Jones). This type of surveillance may lend to why Black girls are quick to have their guard up, against all who partake in monitoring them.

Limited research has been devoted specifically to Black females, but a study by Lei (2003) looks at how some Black girls self-identity can cause them to develop an attitude that displays relationally aggressive tactics that could turn into violence. Lei (2003), examines the characterizations of people of color and the process of identity construction in the creation of students as academic and social beings. A main focus was on how students constructed their own identity, responded with strategic acts, resistance, conformity, and disruption to the regulatory system (Lei, p. 159). Black girls were focused on because patterns emerged that pointed to specific and prevailing representations that did not emerge in other races of students. Lei (2003), felt that there would be significant implications for race relations and academic achievements for students at the host High School. According to Lei (2003), much research has been devoted to African American males, but little attention has been given to African American females in the scholarly research realm. Judith Butler (1990, 1993) works on complex interactions are used to provide the theoretical value between the subject, the body, and identity. A rudimentary explanation of the theory is an evolution of time develops individuals who believe they are supposed to look, act, and sound a certain way. Therefore, they conform and follow suit.

Lei conducted her study at Hope High School (HH) which is situated in a medium sized city of Jackson in the Midwest. The school has a population of 1,776 students. Sixty-eight percent of the students were white, 18.5 percent were Black, 8.5 percent Asian American, 4.3 percent were Hispanic, and 0.5 percent was American Indian. The diverse population at HH was also represented by a wide range of socio-economics. Twenty-five percent of students were eligible for free or reduced lunch. The "Black girls" were categorized as loud and tough. An immediate question that ponders may be a potentially researchable problem, which is; will the behaviors or the perception of "Black girls" be the same or different if the majority of the students were Black? Lei interviewed many different students at HH on or about experiences with "Black girls" (BG). In one account, a Cambodian student was interviewed on an account where a 2 BG were standing in the hallway and a White male walks in front of the BG. One BG responds by snapping at the boy and jacking him up, saying he better not walk in front of her. The Cambodian student could not understand what the White male did wrong, only that the one BG snapped. An analysis is provided that explains the BG reaction as a sense of power in this situation and a need to be respected, but onlookers did not see the White male as creating subordination to the BG.

When placed in a socio-historical context the negative loudness of the BG represents a historical set of norms created by mass society as the antithesis of White female culture and image (Fordham, 1993). Lei (2003), makes a reference that the BG "loudness" is attributed as a way to assert their power and be recognized. At HH, the BG were disciplined for their loud behaviors that were categorized as negative. One student that Lei (2003) interviewed developed a means of "code switching", which is the ability to speak appropriately for the appropriate occasions. As the student learned this art, she became more accepted by all individuals, because she felt she behaved in a less threatening manner. Lei (2003), goes on to say that authoritative figures need to understand that the way they react to the behaviors have consequences for the student's academic achievement. Lei (2003) recommend an institution of cultural practices, so the norms of "race, sex, gender, and sexuality" aren't artificially imposed. This occurrence is an example of how relational aggression in Black females may be a unique experience due to their identity construction. Currently, it is unknown how urban adolescent Black females construct their identity online and how cyberbullying, a form of relational aggression can escalate to conflict in an urban school environment due to their unique perspectives and experiences.

CHAPTER SUMMARY

This review of the literature review has illuminated that cyberbullying a form of relational aggression, "is an evolution of ways in which kids beat each other up" (McQuade et al., p. 13). The research on cyberbullying shows a need for continuous study of this topic, due to the prevalence and rates in which it is occurring. Cyberbullying represents a fast emerging movement within the Digital Youth Culture that may need further examination, especially in those areas where gaps in the literature exist. When examining the literature, there has been little to no representation of Black females and their experiences with cyberbullying, or no nationally educationally governed body of literature that implores why violent incidents among Black females occur in school. Chapter 3 of this dissertation will provide the methodology that will be used to study adolescent Black females and their experiences with cyberbullying in an urban high school.

CHAPTER 3

METHODOLOGY

Chapter 3 presents the methodology that guided this qualitative research study. The context and setting of this study will be explored, and the data collection and analysis methods will be explained. The remains of the chapter explain the methods in which data was stored, managed, and maintained. Lastly, a research timeline will show the progression of this research study. This study addressed how Black adolescent females experience cyberbullying. If they were victimized, what were their experiences?

RESEARCH METHODOLOGY

This study adopted a phenomenological approach to understanding the experiences Black adolescent females have with cyberbullying as participants and victims. According to Creswell (2003), qualitative research may be applied when: (a) the topic is relatively new, (b) the important aspects of the phenomenon are unknown, and (c) discourse was not given to a specific group of people. Currently, studying Black females' experiences with cyberbullying in an urban environment meets all three criteria. Patchin and Hinduja (2006) support the notion that cyberbullying is a newer phenomenon, which has not received adequate attention from academia, specifically from the perspective of race and gender.

This study used a phenomenological approach to investigate urban Black adolescent females' experiences as participants and victims of cyberbullying because limited discourse has been given to this population. Much of the research on cyberbullying has taken a quantitative approach and given monologue to affluent suburban Caucasian females (Epstein & Kazmierczack, 2007). This study used this phenomenological approach as an interpretive method to study how groups of people (Black females) react to similar phenomena in order to increase awareness about the effects of those phenomena (Van Manen, 1990).

According to Miles and Huberman (1994), the researcher must identify the parts of the phenomenon which are not well understood. One salient example is the lack of understanding regarding the effects of cyberbullying on Black adolescent females in an urban high school. Research supports that relational aggression has the potential to turn into violent conflict among Black females due to adverse living conditions (USDHHS, 2001), but cyberbullying a form of relational aggression is currently unknown how it affects urban Black females in school. Conducting this phenomenological study provided meaning to the phenomenon and provides depth to lived experiences (Cottrell & McKenzie, 2005).

STUDY SETTING

This research was conducted in the Fidelity Central School District (FCSD), which is a large urban district in upstate New York. Serving approximately 35,000 racially and ethnically diverse students, FCSD is composed of 64 percent African-American, 22 percent Hispanic, 11 percent Caucasian, and 3 percent Asian. Also, with 84 percent of students receiving free or reduced lunch, FCSD reports the worst poverty of the five largest districts in the state.

Additionally, the FCSD reports a high rate of student suspensions; but, with its "no out of school suspensions" policy, those suspended students are kept off the city streets and on school grounds during the school day. When the data for the 2008-2009 school year was released, the FCSD disclosed approximately 7,000 instances of in-school suspension (ISS) issued at the secondary high school level. Approximately 2,500 issues stemmed from conflict such as intimidation, harassment, menacing, bullying, minor altercations, and assaults with physical injury. The reports also identified almost 4,000 incidents that resulted from other disruptive incidents, which may or may not have included conflict. Black students accounted for approximately 5,260 ISS issuances and females accounted for a total of 2,500 such instances (Fidelity City School District [FCSD], 2009). The data was not broken up by race and gender. The FCSD data confirms that significant issues have resulted from conflict, but the data does not represent what the conflict was or why it began. Therefore, presenting a need to understand the experiences and origins of the conflict, this study will specifically explore if and how cyberbullying plays a role in creating or fostering conflict.

This research will be conducted at Monticello High School (MHS) in FCSD. MHS was a comprehensive high school throughout its years in existence until the 2009-2010 school year. MHS, composed of approximately 1,100 students, currently consists of three Small Learning Communities that specialize in Health Science, Entrepreneurship, and the Arts. According to School Digger (2006-2009), the ethnic breakdown included approximately 750 Black, 150 Hispanic, 135 Caucasian, 73 Asian, and six Native American students. MHS's free and reduced lunch rate, which measures the poverty index, is 93 percent, which is higher than the FCSD's district average. The average annual salary of the school's surrounding neighborhood is $18,000 (Neighborhood Link, 1997-2009).

During the 2008-2009 school year, MHS had approximately 460 students receive In-School-Suspension (ISS) due to various offenses. Upwards of 80 suspensions issued stemmed from conflict areas including intimidation, harassment, menacing, bullying, minor altercations, and assaults with physical injury. The remainder of suspensions came from the category of, "Other Disruptive Incidents" that may, or may not, have stemmed from conflict. Black students accounted for 318 suspensions and females accounted for a total of 120 suspensions. More recent data provided by MSH for the 2010-2011 school year shows that the school had approximately 40 incidents resulting in suspensions within a three month period. The data was not representative of race and gender.

The researcher is an employee of Monticello High School with access to demographic data as well as all information regarding suspensions. The researcher has been an Assistant Principal at MHS for six school years, and currently leads a Small Learning Community composed of students in grades seven through twelve, thus facilitating student access. None of the participants in this study were under the direct supervision of the researcher, which was purposely done to eliminate any conflicts of interest.

PARTICIPANT RECRUITMENT

After the Internal Review Board (IRB) approval was received from St. John Fisher College and the FCSD, the researcher began by selecting 10 participants. The researcher initially utilized professional networking contacts with other administrators within MHS in order to establish a list of Black females that met the preliminary requirements for participation in the researcher's study. After formulating the initial list, the researcher accessed the district's information system and verified the participants' (a) age; (b) gender; (c) ethnicity; (d) at least one suspension on their record, due to a conflict. The specific categories which helped inform the researcher included intimidation, harassment, menacing and bullying, minor altercations, and assaults with physical injury. Additionally, the participants in this study had active FaceBook pages.

PARTICIPANT CRITERIA

Purposeful sampling was utilized to identify participants for this study who illuminated the experiences of urban Black adolescent females regarding cyberbullying, victimization, and the convergence of relational aggression to face-to-face conflict. Participants who were at least 18 years of age were selected because they had a vast array of experiences in high school and were able to reflect on the different experiences, which have caused them conflict or interruptions to their educational process by losing valuable learning time due to suspension. Ten Black females were chosen from the school's database in which an aggressive altercation was indicated.

The researcher viewed their discipline history for insight into the type of "conflict" or "minor altercation" they have experienced, informing the selection process. The justification for one suspension, due to a conflict, demonstrated that the participant was affected by an engagement of negative interactions with her peers. Therefore, this study provided an opportunity to learn if the conflict was related to cyberbullying and the experiences resulting from it. As students were selected, they were each asked if they had a Facebook page and if they were willing to discuss private information regarding their conversations. All of the individuals selected were willing to share their personal information and private Facebook conversations.

PARTICIPANT OVERVIEW

Upon selection of the 10 students, a letter to participants (Appendix A) was given to the students. The letter provided the following information: (a) a brief overview of the study; (b) date and time for the first general meeting; and (c) an interview schedule for participants. The first meeting was brief, and it focused on reviewing the overview of the study and securing participant signatures for consent forms (Appendix B). The participants were provided with a one-page document summarizing the study and participant expectations (Appendix C). Next, the participants were asked to complete a demographic profile sheet which provided the researcher with a baseline understanding of the participants' Internet usage habits (Appendix D). See table 3.1 for a sample of questions and answers.

TABLE 3.1

DEMOGRAPHIC PROFILE SHEET DATA

Participant Name	Time Spent Online	Favorite Social Networking Activity	Verbal Argument at School Due to FB	Physical Altercation at School Due to FB
1-Keisha	15 hours	Gaming	Often	0
2-Tia	7 hours	Posting on others pages	Sometimes	0
3-Charmaine	1 hours	Gaming	Once	1-3
4-Danielle	2 hours	Posting on others pages	Once	0
5-Jane	30 min	Posting comment on own page	Once	0
6-Ashley	15 hours	Posting on others pages	Never	0
7-Kate	2 hours	Gaming	Never	0
8-Anai	13 hours	Blogging	Sometimes	0
9-Harriet	3 hours	Blogging	Never	0
10-Alisha	5 hours	Chatting	Never	0

The students were urged to go home and notify their parents of their participation in the study, even though parental consent was not mandatory, as the participants were at least 18 years of age. The ensuing meetings facilitated the individual interviews which focused heavily on the participants experience with social networking. These interviews generated insight into the different elements of conflict for the purpose of analysis.

The students who participated were linked to MHS's Student Family Support Center (SFSC) in case counseling was needed. The SFSC, a facility that houses different agencies, provides free mental health support to the schools' students. An agreement was made (Appendix E) with the SFSC to check in on each student after their interview (Appendix F) in order to ensure that counseling was provided if needed. Each student had access to a mental health counselor due to the possibility that discussing this topic could rehash previous conflict-rich situations.

DATA COLLECTION

Four data gathering techniques that were utilized include: (a) demographic profile sheets; (b) semi-structured interviews; (c) field notes; and, (d) document collection. The four forms of data were interwoven and utilized to assist in exploring the experiences of cyberbullying, relational aggression, and conflict among the study's participants.

Demographic profile sheet. Illustrated in the table above, the demographic profile sheet (DPS) (Appendix D) consisted of preliminary questions that were disseminated and answered during the initial meeting. The DPS was used to gain demographical and Internet usage information, and gather preliminary information regarding the participants' Internet access, usage, Facebook usage, and self-reported history with in-school violence and conflicts. Upon collection of the DPS, the researcher assigned pseudonyms to each participant in order to maintain confidentiality. The pseudonym identified the participant throughout the remainder of the study.

Semi-structured interviews. The phenomenon of cyberbullying among urban adolescent Black females was investigated further through semi-structured interviews. Semi-structured interviews (Appendix F) conducted individually provided the participants an opportunity to open up and disclose information without fear. The interview questions were open-ended, allowing the participants to honestly express their experiences with cyberbullying.

All interview sessions were held at MHS during the summer months. The researcher worked with the participants to identify the best meeting times to ensure that the participants' were interrupted from their daily schedules as little as possible. The 10 semi-structured interviews were conducted over a two week period and were held in a secure office, ensuring privacy for the participants. The initial interview session lasted for approximately one hour and the researcher scheduled a second round of interviews as a follow-up, in the event that the participants wished to share additional information. None of the participants ended up needing to interview more than once because all questions were answered satisfactorily during the first interview.

The rationale for conducting semi-structured interviews, instead of other qualitative techniques, was because of the sensitive nature of the material. The researcher was aware that the questions posed to each participant could indirectly implicate other participants within the study. Utilizing a one-on-one method ensured that the participants' answers did not ignite any old situations, causing an immediate reaction. The interview sessions began by discussing the DPS, which facilitated conversation and eased the participants into deeper, open-ended questions. Secondly, the open-ended questions were used to facilitate rich dialogue about past experiences. Lastly, the interviews were concluded by allowing the participants to ask questions of the researcher.

The interviews were recorded by using an audio-recorder that plugs into the wall. Additionally, an external digital recorder was used as a backup device to ensure successful data collection. All interviews were transcribed within a three day period by a professional transcriptionist recommended by the St. John Fisher staff.

Field notes. Field notes included handwritten notes collected during the various forms of data collection. They provided immediate feedback for improving the process. After each interview field notes were reviewed and modifications to interview questions occurred when necessary. The researcher noted if particular questions were confusing and if changes of any sort were necessary. Additionally, the field notes documented verbal and non-verbal gestures, along with any other displayed emotions or biases. Field notes were also taken when the documentation collection was discussed with the participants. These notes provide insight as to the participants' experiences with cyberbullying and social networking.

Document collection. The participant's school disciplinary behavior history was collected and analyzed to verify the student's answers to Demographic Profile Sheet questions. Additionally, the student's age, gender, and ethnicity were collected and stored in a binder.

DATA ANALYSIS

Data analysis was ongoing and occurred throughout the data collection process, ensuring continuous improvement as the study progressed (Marshall & Rossman, 2011). The information was processed, and a systematic approach was taken to ensure that appropriate themes and categories were created and aligned accordingly with the research questions. The analytic procedures which fall into seven stages set the framework for the data analysis process: (a) organizing the data; (b) immersion into the data; (c) generating pre-existing codes; (d) applying codes to the data; (e) interpreting the data; (f) developing alternative understandings; and (g) writing a report or presenting the study (Marshall & Rossman, 2011, p. 209). This framework reduced an immense amount of data to a manageable state, allowing the researcher to do meaningful interpretations of the information collected. The following sections will describe each of the seven analytical stages.

The organization of the data was continuous and last until the completion of the study. The researcher organized the data electronically and through printed hard copies. A table was created using Microsoft Excel to assist the researcher with tracking and organizing the research data. The table list: (a) pseudonym; (b) GPA; and (c) answers to all the DPS questions. This log was maintained throughout the study's entirety. All hard copy information was placed in binders that included the DPS, participant disciplinary information, transcriptions, field notes, and it was all separated by participant. The electronic data was stored on the researcher's personal computer and on an external hard drive.

The researcher read and re-read the data and repeatedly listened to the audio recordings (Marshall & Rossman, 2011). The researcher became intimate with the data in order to establish a familiarity, or immersion, that facilitated a heightened level of understanding. To improve understanding of the data, the researcher established codes and themes from the reoccurring language and ideas specified by the participants. The codes were developed by using the theoretical framework of relational aggressions to formulate categories that coincided with the research questions. The theory generated codes were relationships, conflict, identity, and popularity, which were all placed in a Microsoft Word table.

First level coding was conducted to find reoccurring themes and relationships amongst theory and real-life data. The researcher coded to create attributes from the described phenomenon (Miles & Huberman, 1994). The researcher bracketed and labeled important words, ideas, phrases, and sentences to identify any patterns; which helped establish a secondary level of coding. The precisely created codes used abbreviated titles developed by the researcher. Ultimately, 32 codes were derived from the data. A code sheet was created by using a Microsoft Word table. The code sheet consisted of the participants' pseudonym and each code that presented itself in their individual interview. Additionally, the participants' spoken words helped to develop invivo codes; these codes are terms that emerged from the real-life data (Marshall & Rossman, 2011).

Upon the appearance of master codes, the researcher created a clear operational definition of each code (Miles & Huberman), ensuring consistency over the course of the study. The researcher explored all of the codes to look for anticipated relationships between the data as well as unexpected affiliations. Once themes emerged, they were narrowed down to a manageable, hierarchal state that was linked to the theoretical framework on relational aggression (Ryan & Bernard, 2003). The codes started to establish patterns that highlighted the experiences of Black adolescent females with cyberbullying, which aided in the achievement of further understanding the phenomenon.

The researcher initially examined the pre-existing codes as related to the theoretical framework, the research problem, and research questions. Next, the researcher established additional codes, in addition to the pre-existing codes in order to establish themes. The themes were a result of patterns and relationships that resulted from the four forms of data. Then, the researcher used Microsoft One Note to piece together information from the transcripts that seemed to follow similar patterns. It was comparative to putting together a puzzle, carefully aligning data to form a picture of analysis.

Thematic memos were written under each piece of data to aid with the understanding and organization process. The notes represented an initial attempt to piece a story together by keeping analytical notes. According to Marshall and Rossman (2011), writing can help the analyst to develop initial codes and create linkages among further coded data. The researcher searched for explanations and made inferences regarding the data to begin imposing meaning. The story was examined to unravel the social phenomenon.

The data was examined for alternative meanings. Once saturation of the data occurred and patterns emerged repeatedly, the researcher scrutinized the collected information, looking for faulty approaches, and early mistakes (Marshall & Rossman, 2011). This portion of analysis focused on finding information that did not emerge from the initial coding process. The researcher coded and compiled a list of alternate meanings from each form of data and used it to develop alternate themes. Establishing alternative understanding can facilitate future associations between the most apparent findings and less obvious correlations. The researcher developed an understanding of the research that is not initially noticeable while interpreting the data.

Writing the thematic memos was an integral aspect of the summarization process. The memos and the coded data developed a story of common experiences that Black adolescent females have endured due to cyberbullying in an urban environment. The researcher ascribed meaning to the data that was collected from the DPS, semi-structured interviews, field notes, and documentation collection process, taking care to create a summation of written analysis that does not impose his voice within the findings. The researcher presented all of the findings accurately without limiting them to an individual perspective. The researcher continuously analyzed the data throughout the study to ensure that the final written analysis was in tune with the true language that presents itself from the research. Trustworthiness was obtained by participating in the seven steps identified previously, allowing the data to be collected and analyzed with efficiency.

TRUSTWORTHINESS

Triangulation can occur when three or more data sources are utilized to juxtapose the participants' perspectives. When multiple data sources are used, the accuracy of the research study increases (Creswell, 2003). This study used four different forms of qualitative data: (a) demographic profile sheets; (b) semi-structured interviews; (c) field notes; and (d) document collection. The researcher used the same process to interview and organize the information for all 10 participants. Additionally, the researcher established inter-rater reliability by having a seasoned qualitative researcher code a portion of the transcripts. Similar results were established. Code and data quality checks were made in order to ensure adequate agreement and to account for any bias or deceit (Miles & Huberman). Research was conducted over a reasonable timeline and related back to the research questions.

STUDY LIMITATIONS

Initially, the study was designed so the ten participants would have to allow the researcher to view their social networking pages, in order to view an authentic conversation that would provide insight into whether the students are participants or victims of cyberbullying. The researcher had to eliminate this portion of the document collection process due to the IRB. The IRB felt that reviewing the participants Facebook pages would infringe upon their privacy. This form of documentation would have been useful for this study because social networking is important to adolescent development, as it represents a social space where adolescents convene to rally for popularity and social status (Hinduja & Patchin, 2008). The collection of this form of data could have been valuable because it would have provided real world examples of conflict and, upon analysis; it could have provided triangulation with the answers from the interview. Additionally, prior to conducting the interviews, the researcher printed, reviewed, analyzed, and secured data regarding the participants' incident and suspension history.

CHAPTER SUMMARY

The goal of this phenomenological study is to unearth feelings and notions that participants have regarding their experiences with cyberbullying and how it may have affected their high school experience (Cottrell & McKenzie, 2005). The information was transcribed, coded, and then entered into a matrix. This process assisted the researcher with organizing the data for reporting the results in Chapter 4 and writing implications in Chapter 5.

CHAPTER 4

FINDINGS

Chapter 4 reports the findings of this study, which are derived from the guiding research questions: How do urban Black adolescent females describe their experiences as participants and victims of cyberbullying? If they were victimized, what were their experiences? This chapter also identifies four relevant themes and describes them in terms of online identity, relationships, conflict, and conflict resolution. The findings are interrelated and will clarify how urban Black adolescent females experience cyberbullying. This chapter concludes with the development of strategies for reducing and eliminating online and in-person conflict.

STUDY FINDINGS

Throughout the findings, an illumination of power positioned itself within all four themes. Power was demonstrated by an ability to control and use variations of mental strength to influence others. Power was used as a form of bullying among the various themes. Often, it exemplified itself covertly through relational aggressive tactics such as rumors, slanderous remarks, or an elimination of friendships. Ultimately, strategies were developed by the participants to position themselves as tougher than their peers, and more socially adept. The goals were to reduce their chance of experiencing verbal and physical victimization while simultaneously increasing their social status on and offline.

FB THUGGIN: ELEVATED SOCIAL STATUS

The first theme discussed in this chapter, "Facebook (FB) Thuggin: Elevated Social Status." A term that is popular with the majority of this study's participants, as the young women described how Facebook facilitates thuggish behavior. The participants shared that this form of bullying behavior was often enacted to position themselves as powerful beings, which were unafraid of verbal tirades and physical threats. The term also categorized participants' beliefs that online identities allow girls to act differently than they do in person. Appearing tougher online than their normal in-person personas, allows users to gain attention and achieve social prowess among their online peers.

This first theme creates a distinction between online and real world behavior. When asked to elaborate and provide examples of "FB Thuggin," the majority of the participants described the acts of peers, rather than recalling their own similar actions. Often, the participants defined and described "Facebook Thuggin" in broad terms, which suggests that they do not take responsibility for their actions, but know others who create such facades.

"FB Thuggin" is enacted to gain popularity by creating a false persona. The majority of the participants felt that portraying themselves as tough would make people want to be with them instead of against them, thus displaying their power, and building their social status. Social networking sites allow their users, including this study's participants, to build their social capital. Danielle, an 18-year-old Junior whose favorite online activity is to post on others' social networking pages, uses Facebook to elevate her social status. During Danielle's interview, she described FB Thuggin as: "Like you getting on somebody's page talking junk, like negative things, like oh when I see you I'm going to beat you up or some stuff like that, bullying, cyber bullying". Danielle indicated that she demonstrates a tough online persona to prove that she is not someone who is easily bullied, without sticking up for herself.

Danielle wants respect and believes that the more well known she is, the more respect she will have. Danielle feels that portraying herself as a tough individual online has increased her level respect and improved her social capital. According to Danielle, "FB Thuggin" contributes to online and public social acceptance, which she equates with popularity. She believes that increased online acceptance translates to a decrease in being picked on at school. As Danielle began to gain popularity on Facebook, she described how the use of "FB Thuggin" allowed her to feel good about herself, saying: "Nobody really shows me respect, to be honest, in person, so I don't really show many people respect when I'm online in Facebook. I say what I want to say and I say what I feel."

She presents it as if she does not deserve respect and, in return, she is not going to give it, either. Somewhere in her development, she has acquired a poor self-image; but, hurting others' feelings online is a way of diverting attention toward others, away from her own insecurities. Her hope in utilizing this self-defense mechanism is to prevent herself from being categorized as a victim. Additionally, Danielle shared that she can be shy in person, and that Facebook has given her an outlet for enhancing her level of comfort in social situations, which, in return, has made her more popular.

Social Networking has improved my identity. I have more respect. Because like when people get to know me more, they know I'm a cool person, I'm a chill person and I don't do drama. It made me confident. Because of the respect I was getting and people was encouraging me like, you a good friend; yeah I think I should hang with you more, it made you feel good and made you like, you know, you have more confidence than what you had when you didn't have that much friends.

Danielle advised that "FB Thuggin" attracts people to her FB page and caused them to request her as a friend. About the people requesting her, she said: "I didn't really know, but I add them because they sent me a friend request so I add them and then they get to know me from there." She admitted that the encouragement helped her to feel good about herself.

It made me more popular like when more friends or more people starting to talk to you more, people that you wanted to talk to but didn't know what to say and they talk to you first, that's like, that makes you feel good. Because you won't be all fearful, you won't be all shy, you know, you're behind the computer and they behind the computer.

She appears to be less guarded online because she feels popular and has aligned herself with people who will boost her self-esteem. Ultimately, Danielle feels more powerful due to a decrease in disrespect and an elevation in her social status. FB Thuggin also assumes fake identities; it positions its characters as social actors among their peers to elevate attractiveness and reduce victimization.

Other participants, such as Kiesha, describe "FB Thuggin" as people being something that they are not in real life. Kiesha, a senior who carried a 3.0 GPA, found herself involved in physical altercations due to social networking. According to Keisha, Facebook is filled with people who are not honest about who they really are in school or community settings.

Oh my gosh, because they pretend to be something that they're not. Like behind the computer screen, they feel like they're just superior to everybody, based on when you're with your friends like outside of Facebook and the Internet and stuff they're like different, more laid back and more like honest with themselves. But when they get on Facebook they create a whole other identity. You could be anybody on Facebook.

Thus, Kiesha believed that people participate in "FB Thuggin" to embellish what they are in real life in order to increase their social status. Ashley, a 19-year-old graduating senior, who has been in physical altercations due to FB, agrees with Kiesha. Ashley states, "'Cause some people portray their self as being like this big tough person online when in all actuality they're just the softest little person you ever seen, or just a scary person." Ashley clarifies that the individual's true identity does not match their online persona, but their self-portrait has created an attractive personification that exudes confidence. They have an outlet where they can endeavor to reinvent themselves and enhance the attractiveness of their inner being.

Anai, who admittedly desires to be popular online and currently has over 3,000 FB friends, reported spending 13 hours a day, online. She, too, described individuals within her social network that use FB as a vehicle to drive popularity, Particularly by the opposite gender. Apparently, presenting oneself as a tough individual is considered attractive within this particular peer group, and is representative of the old expression: "chicks dig bad boys."

Oh, Facebook Thuggin means people who are on Facebook they think they tough on Facebook, but they're really not like that in real life. They try to bully and stuff on Facebook or they try to be like oh I'm tough or whatever like, there's so many people like they don't have any affiliations with any gangs or anything like that, but on Facebook like you see all these pictures with all these flags and they putting up all these gang signs and then like you know in real life this person is not selling no drugs, this person is not in no gang, this person has never been in a fight and won. But, like they try to put that kind of image on Facebook because they think maybe okay it'll attract more girls. Whatever; and increase my popularity somehow.

Throughout Anai's interview, she alludes that girls like to associate themselves with boys who appear to be popular on and offline because it heightens the girls social status. Conversely, not many girls admitted that they directly participated in FB Thuggin.

Of the ten interviews, only one participant directly admitted to "FB Thuggin." The other nine participants described how others utilized "FB Thuggin," or hinted to their participation. Kate, an 18-year-old junior, who spends approximately two hours a day online, was the lone participant who took ownership of her acts of "FB Thuggin."

When I'm online, I see a lot of comments that upset me so I'll naturally react to them. Like I comment against them badly, you know, you type your little comment up there, you know, I respond like I'm crazy, but the person will come back into school and oh yeah I'll do this and that, and so it will be different. But in the real world outside of the cyber world as they call it, I'm very more towards my caring and loving buddy type person.

Kate admits that through "FB Thuggin" she reacts a little tougher than she would react in person. In person, she says that her reactions are more in keeping with her true, caring self. The online arena enables her to respond in a way that may be typically out of character. During the interview, the majority of participants conveyed that they did not want to be referred to as phony or fake, so they said they maintained a consistent persona, behaving the same way whether online or not. However, their other answers belied their tendency to change their identity online in order to portray themselves in a light that may allow them to gain popularity, respect, or street credibility. As Kate noted, "FB Thuggin" is predicated upon a lack of balance between real world and cyber-identities.

Some people spend so much time on the Internet they forget that they have a life outside of it. They go there and they do all of their living online, they forget what it means to be, you know, what it is to live outside of the Internet and they just forget. They bring their online swagger to the real world and they just forget, oh it's just a fake identity and then they try and project it as themselves and it just gets ridiculous.

Her statement supports her belief that that many individuals forget who they really are because the Internet enables them to morph into whoever they want to be. "FB Thuggin" is a tool designed by the participants to increase attractiveness to the opposite sex, and to elevate social status, which in return provides a sense of security, because popularity was viewed as a way to shield from victimization. Thus, "FB Thuggin" provides insight into the development of the other three themes within this study.

MOVING TOO FAST: RELATIONSHIPS WITHOUT SUBSTANCE

The second theme, "Moving Too Fast: Relationships without Substance," was created to illustrate how quickly friendships can be formed online without the benefit of establishing the otherwise requisite bond of trust. As described by the participants, relationships are easier to form online because online users can idealize or exaggerate their traits, which can be intriguing, yet dishonest. Participants further describe how dishonesty ruins relationships, preventing true friendships from forming. The participants who displayed more boundaries, as demonstrated by limiting additions of FB friends were also less worried about their social status, decreasing their chances for conflict online and at school.

Participants described the nature of online relationships. Many of the FB relationships that are formed by this study's participants are characterized as relationships without substance. Often, an FB friendship is formed by accepting a friend request that is sent by an unknown individual. These relationships are formed quickly and in large numbers. For example, Alisha a recent high school graduate, who spends five hours online stated; "I have like 300 Facebook friends, but out of them 300, I probably like talk to like 10." She suggests that she only regularly converses with 10 of her FB friends because she does not really have a true bond of friendship with the other 290 individuals. The speed in which relationships are formed does not allow for trust to be established among social networkers. The participants in this study discussed how their personal life details, shared online, were often used by someone within their network to create conflict.

Obviously, friends in good standing do not try to harm one another. Yet, the data from this study shows that the majority of the participants' social networks were composed of individuals with limited connections beyond cyberspace. Overwhelmingly, the participants discussed that they trusted their real world friends more than their online friends. Jane, who enjoys meeting new friends online states; "Because people on Facebook don't really know you." Thus, Jane iterated that face-to-face time needs to be spent with friends in order to develop trustful relationships. Additionally, some of the participants' networks were so immense that knowing everyone with which they are connected is not plausible. The participants in this study ranged from girls who have five FB friends to girls that have over 3000 FB friends. Among the participants, the Internet was often described as a social meeting space that becomes a haven for fake identities and relationships built on untruths and misconceptions.

Tia, a 19-year-old second-year senior, reveals that she frequently gets into arguments on FB, and she has been in at least one physical altercation due to FB. She expresses difficulty with forming relationships online, citing a lack of online privacy, which is exacerbated as the number of a user's FB friends increases. While an individual's FB page can be marked as private, an individual with over 700 friends can create a virtual high school with their page and all of their online friends can witness and contribute to the posts that comprise the participant's wall, which is commonly their personal business.

Yeah, it makes it worse because people get involved in your business. People try to figure out what was going on and you got the people that's trying to be nosey and gossip and things getting transferred to one another and the wrong words being said. So when it's out in public it does make it worse.

Tia has over 700 friends on Facebook and often she feels that her online posts are misunderstood and that her friends confuse her words, gossiping against her. The public nature of Facebook impedes the development of genuine relationships between potential friends. A myriad of opinions are constantly voiced through online communication, and they often are misconstrued. Once the message is posted, the entire Facebook community can see it and commence with sharing their varied interpretations and evaluations of the latest FB post, the results of which, the study's participants believe, will affect their social standing. Ashley, who has a 1.85 GPA and uses the Internet for approximately 15 hours a day, proclaims that her page is private, but yet she has over 800 FB friends. Ashley goes on to say that, of her 800 FB friends, 20 of them, a group of her schoolmates, would be considered friends outside of Facebook.

I'd say about a good 800 or so Facebook friends. My page is private. Because yeah it's a way to meet friends but you don't just want everybody in your business. Because regardless if you're online or not people still are not going to be honest with you, keep it real, it could be somebody you need to talk to or whatever, or they could lie, stab you in the back, still do sneaky stuff.

Ashley believes that, if a person is a liar, they will lie whether in person or online. She desires popularity, yet she purports to value her privacy. Conversely, Ashley advises that she is careful when selecting FB friends because she knows that they would have access to her page; yet she has 800 friends. Ashley has enough friends on her page to populate a high school. Ashley's FB page should not be considered a private place. The fact that she only considers a small portion of her total FB friends list as actual friends indicates that Ashley's thirst for popularity is overriding her desire for privacy. While emphasizing the importance of relationships and her wish to develop them privately, her actions indicate an unspoken emphasis on achieving popularity. She wants to be liked but admits that she does not trust anyone, online or otherwise. Ashley additionally states:

I hang with about 20 facebook friends in school. Because I know them like I actually been in class myself with them and so hung out with them in school and outside of school, so I know how they are compared to the people that just send me friend requests and we just chat online. So I actually know how my 20 friends are.

Initially, Ashley said FB and real world friends were the same. However, as further questions were presented, she seemed to become aware of the differences between the two types of friends. Ashley's example showed that she actually has a relationship with 20 out of 800 people, which further supports that real world friends quite differ from cyberfriends. The accounts of each participant's experiences support the assertion that real world friends are considered to be more sincere than FB friends.

Unequivocally shared among the participants was the idea that, even though relationships on FB may not be as rich or real, it is easier to get to know someone online because they are emboldened by a sense of online anonymity. Jane is a recent graduate who reports spending approximately 30 minutes a day online and uses FB to meet new friends and post comments on her own page. She shares insight into why it may be easier to make friends on Facebook than in the real world.

Sometimes people on Facebook understand more than real friends that you have and see every day. Because people on Facebook don't really know you so they don't really go and tell people what you tell them, but people that go to school with you they go to everybody in the whole school.

Due to having less of a real world connection with Facebook friends, it is easier for her to talk to them and share information. Additionally, a person may have ulterior motives for acquiring an FB friend, and they may be pretending to relate to a person's posts in order to exploit the resulting confidence. For example, someone with a false identity may act and speak as a friend in order to collect information and use it as gossip. Jane, along with many others, feels that sharing personal information with a real friend can be harder than sharing on FB, because real friends may apply knowledge of prior events to alter their interpretation of the admission and that they may be more personally invested in the information than FB friends. She is afraid that individuals at school will share intimate details of her life with fellow classmates. Ironically, the information travels faster and fosters more gossip than could possibly be achieved if spread within the walls of a school building.

Even though Jane stated earlier that she finds it easier to share personal information with her FB friends, she realizes that individuals lie about themselves online and, as a result, relationships do not fully develop into friendships, because full disclosure is not happening. In school, friends can see a person's actions, reactions, and mannerisms. However, the online arena is comprised entirely of the words a person chooses to write, and the reader must interpret the meaning without the benefit of the aforementioned actions, reactions, and mannerisms. There are no other indicators to tell whether the writer is truthful.

It's different because the people online they like go to different schools and they're from other places and the people in school are the people that you hang out with is different because you see them every day, and like people online they lie about who they are so they think you're this person and you're really not. So people at school know who you really are that's the difference, for me that's the difference.

Throughout the study, many of the participants divulge that real world relationships are different from FB relationships because trust is not easily established online. Virtually every participant stated that non-verbal communication; which helps an individual determine whether their friends are lying, is chief among the factors that determine a real world relationship. Alisha, a recent graduate who states she avoids online conflict so much that she recently deleted her FB account, agrees that non-verbal communication assists with determining whether a friend is being truthful.

Facebook friends tell you like tell you what they think you want to hear cause it's over Facebook, it's not like they're telling it to you in your face, they could just lie to you, lie to you, and lie to you and make you believe it, but as far as being in your face you could basically tell when your friends are lying to you face-to-face or not. Because on the computer you could like I said before you could just write anything without people viewing your body language and tell how you really react to a certain conversation or something.

Six out of ten interviewees mentioned the importance of body language when forming sincere trustful relationships. Each participant who referenced the importance of non-verbal communication agreed that trust cannot be fully achieved without face-to-face conversations. According to Ashley, "I don't know, I think it's because if you actually say it to a person then they could like see it in your face or whatever, the seriousness or the sincerity that you have." Because body language is not available online, the participants compensate by being less trusting when interacting online.

Without body language, the overwhelming consensus is that many individuals are not completely truthful on FB. Harriet states, "I guess it's the fact that you can't really see the person you're writing to on Facebook, but in the real world you're talking to them face-to-face." It is easier for this participant to form true relationships in person rather than online because people are able to see her and become familiar with her expressions and mannerisms, an opinion that is consistent among most of the girls. Some have said that it may be easier, initially, to talk to someone you do not know, but most true friendships are formed in the real world. Kate says, "In person, people can see me and know the sound of my voice and know my faithful expressions and when I'm being sarcastic or annoying because I shift my eyes when I just don't care."

Two of the ten participants discussed what they believed to be thriving, positive relationships on FB. They contributed such success to keeping a small, intimate, social network, based on family and close, real world friends. The girls who had less FB friends admitted to a lack of concern for popularity. They only used FB as a tool to stay in communication with their real world friends and family. Charmaine, a graduated 18-year-old senior who self-reported that she has never been in a physical fight due to conflict on FB, states that she has never made a derogatory comment about a schoolmate on FB. Additionally, she advised that her FB page is private and that she only accepts friend requests from family members or those with whom she has a pre-existing real world friendship.

I have about 100 FB friends, but it's mainly family. I don't know, it's not something that I like, it's not something that I would like want to be like popular online if we don't talk in person, why would we talk online. See online on like Facebook I only accept people that I talk to regularly. See my page is blocked so no one could find me unless I search for them.

Charmaine keeps her social network intimate, and it has enabled her to minimize the online and in-school conflict that others experience due to online communication. The fact that Charmaine is more discerning with her selections for FB friends has helped her to stay out of online conflict and to reap the advantages of FB with less of the drawbacks. Charmaine provides more insight as to how she uses FB as a communication tool and not as a way to establish extreme popularity.

I think it made some of my relationships stronger. Now that we're not in school, whatever, the person I used to hang out with in school so we don't lose contact we can use, we could talk back and forth on here and meet up and have fun with each other.

FB has been a positive tool for Charmaine, through which she can connect and reconnect with friends. She uses it without opening her personal life up for everyone that requests access. Harriet, an 18-year-old Junior, also self-reports that she strictly uses FB as a tool to communicate with friends, and that, as a result, she has never been in a conflict online. She concurs that getting to know people is easier online than in person, but she elaborates, saying that the true identity of the person may not be as they present it to be upon initially connecting online.

I guess like you could tell the person that you don't really know more about you and stuff. Yeah like you wouldn't be shy to talk to them. But then you can meet that person and think you could already know what that person is about, and they'll portray something to you and then you meet them in person and it's just like ugh, it sucks.

While the participants expressed it was easier to speak to strangers, the young woman also insinuates that online relationships are not based on solid foundations even though they form with a quickness and ease. The participants' immense online networks are another indication of a desire to exude power through popularity. Having large social networks with limited true relationships superficially appear to increase social status, and in some cases it may, but it also has the potential to increase conflict in the participant daily lives as well. Conflict will be discussed in the third theme.

YOU GONNA HAVE TO SEE ME: INVITATION TO FIGHT

The third theme, "You Gonna Have to See Me: Invitation to Fight", describes how online conflict can escalate, causing verbal or physical confrontations at school. "You Gonna Have to See Me," is a phrase that the participants often use to invite another person to a fight. This phrase was commonly used by participants who wish to maintain respect when confronted with an online conflict. For those participants who established social status through high numbers of online friendships, most reported resulting conflict. Often, the participants described how and when they would invite another student to fight due to a conflict that started online. The participants within this study explained that conflict occurred due to several reasons, including increased popularity, a fear of showing weakness, and the need to save face.

The following point of view as described by Kiesha, speaks of a deliberate engagement in online conflict. Keisha, who has received at least one five-day suspension from high school due to a physical altercation, believe that many of her peers create conflict online because they know the rumors will return to school and create a sense of relevancy for themselves in the social realm.

Cause everybody likes drama, so when they see you doing something on Facebook like oh she was arguing with her or she was arguing with her, oh let me be her friend so I can see what she's doing. So you can say that increases your popularity.

Online conflict caused her popularity to increase because she feels that people are attracted to the drama. As reported, social networking allows for more time to socialize than at school, with gossip starting on FB and then playing out at school. Tia, a participant that uses the Internet for approximately seven hours a day to primarily gossip, confirms that conflict occurs online and has increased her popularity. "I say something about something that happened in school that day, or something about somebody, obviously it gets dragged to school the next day."

Her statement confirms that people are following what individuals say online and that it gets brought back to school for resolution. School is often where daily activities occur, and FB is the message board for the discussion of the intimate details of the student's day. Ashley spends the majority of her online time posting on FB pages because she wants others to see what she has to say. In this sense, she seeks social relevance online which often inspires follow-up discussions at school. She said,

A lot of people, I don't know, people like to gossip and things and a lot of that stuff like that. I say how I feel on my statuses or whatever and as people see it and of course all girls like to gossip and start trouble then come back to school with it, and then somebody might like what I said or something and walk around like oh girl you right with that or something like that.

This participant is excited about having others listen to what she has to say, she wants to be heard. She believes that the more people talk about her, the more important she becomes. However, it often carries the price tag of starting conflict with other females.

While Ashley refers to gossip as a normal part of the day, and other participants were not as quick to admit that they purposefully said things to cause conflict and an increase in popularity. This small group of participants was forthcoming, however in describing how gossip spreads quickly and often creates arguments at school. Alisha proclaims a disdain for Facebook and has recently closed her account because she does not want FB drama. She says: "Because it's a lot of drama, people just come to your page to see what you're writing so they could go tell somebody else."

Alisha feels that many people use the site to manufacture conflict where there would otherwise be none. Some individuals allegedly only go to certain people's pages so they can tell someone else what is going on in that person's life. Once they find out the information, a negative spin is placed on it and conflict is created between the individuals. Often, while discussing conflict, the females within this study discussed the importance of maintaining their respect at school, online, and in their neighborhood, by making sure that they do not appear weak in any type of public venue.

Jane admits that whenever someone says something hurtful to her, her first impulse is to physically fight the offender. Jane feels that she cannot display any form of weakness, or people will take advantage of her, and she will lose her social status, becoming fodder for bullies. Jane discusses why maintaining her respect in an urban environment is important to her safety and identity.

I don't want people to think I'm a punk. Because, I don't know, it's not a good image. I'm not the type of person that you can walk over. I say something back. Yeah you get respect cause if you don't say nothing people be like oh you scared, you're a punk, you can't stick up for yourself, so you say something back they know that you stick up for yourself and nobody can't put you down easily.

Jane does not want to be walked on, so she feels that she has to respond aggressively to make sure that everyone watching knows that she should not be taken lightly. By responding to gossip, she is proving herself. Across the interviews, however, such action proves to merely perpetuate the conflict. Girls who seem to be longing for popularity seem more pre-occupied with how others viewed them, reacting to a perceived need to save face in order to maintain their audience's respect. Tia reaffirmed that if someone says anything derogatory to her online or in person and if she chooses not to respond, she fears the social backlash. She discusses how the fear of ridicule is worse than the fear caused by the individual threatening her. Tia said,

I may be afraid, sometimes I could be like if somebody is threatening to jump me I could be worried or like on point of my surroundings, but I'll still come to school cause I don't want to show that I'm like, you know, even if I am scared, I don't want to show that I have any fear inside of me. Yeah it will make it worse like she's a punk, she didn't come to school or like oh I heard she was arguing with this person and they said they were going to beat her up the next day and she didn't come to school.

Tia is unwilling to appear as inferior, and public perception is important to her. It will make her look bad in the eyes of her peers if she is considered to be weak. She may lose her popularity or any status that she has if she appears to be fearful of conflict. Even if she is afraid, she says she will not show it, because she feels that she will become preyed upon. Sticking up for herself and not appearing to be weak was the means to getting other people to leave her alone and exacerbating conflict. It is described as survival of the fittest within the urban environment. When the appearance of not being weak wears off, the female participants describe strategies to save face and maintain their respect. Often, respect is maintained by outdoing others. Power is gained through publically demonstrating fearless aggression. Aggression may be verbal or physical as long as the participant makes it known that they are not afraid or weak. A public perception of toughness can help the participant maintain their social status and safety in an urban environment.

The typical pattern of arguments, as experienced by the participants, usually begins with gossip, rumors, or insults either online or in school. Online is often where the conflict spreads and intensifies. The igniting factors usually occur back and forth, each time one participant will try to outdo the other verbally. There were a total of ten interviews conducted and each participant divulged that they had to save face in at least one situation. If trading rumors or insults were not enough, they would then amp the situation up by inviting the other female or male participant to engage in a physical altercation. Charmaine, who has been in one fight at school, but unrelated to Facebook, describes a situation where her friend misunderstood Charmaine's FB post and turned it into an argument because she did not want to be embarrassed or outdone by Charmaine.

Well once this girl she told me that she wanted to beat me up over something that wasn't true. She told me that, cause I wrote a comment, I wrote a song on my page, I guess she took it the wrong way like I was going after her which I wasn't. It was Fly Above by Candi. It's about overcoming all your obstacles and stuff like that. Yes. It was nothing to do with violence or anything. Then she started posting stuff on Facebook, saying that she's going to beat me up and stuff like that.

The girls used to be friends, but Charmaine's other friend and this girl got into an altercation, so this girl assumed that Charmaine was talking about her. It was a misunderstanding, and the conflict caused an invitation to fight. As reported by Charmaine, the girl demonstrated that she felt disrespected and deemed it necessary to save face by telling Charmaine that she wanted to fight. Ultimately, a fight did not ensue, but real world conflict developed from a posting in cyberspace.

Harriet, another participant who has been in a fight at school, also unrelated to FB, explains an experience where she responded negatively online to a female that she knew did not like her from previous face-to-face meetings.

She didn't like me and I don't know why, she never liked me, and I called her ugly online. So I called her ugly and then, she like she started posted stuff, so I got off my friend's page and stopped posting stuff. She wanted to fight me after I called her ugly online. So it was like I stopped posting stuff with her and just let it go. Yeah, when she seen me she's going to do this and do that. Nothing ever happened, she ended up just stopping.

In many of the interviews, when conflict occurs, the participants go back and forth until someone invites the other to a fight. In this particular situation, Harriet let the situation go and stopped arguing back and forth. Since she refrained from continuing the argument, she explained that the situation stopped, and it never escalated into a physical fight. Since she left her nemesis to argue online by herself, a fight never materialized.

Many of the participants indicated that they had a low tolerance for receiving disrespect online. Danielle, who states that her first response when someone belittles her, is to invite them to fight. Interestingly enough, she admits to never being in a physical altercation due to FB.

I talk junk, I tell them to meet me at a certain place, we can get it in. No, it never happens. I'd say a negative thing like, yo bitch come meet me right now, or you know, just talk my junk basically. Yeah, to resolve it. I don't do all that talking. You don't want everybody to know that you're a scary cat, obviously you want to talk junk back. Talk junk back before, you know, before other friend's see it and they write down a comment. If you don't have respect then basically everybody going to run over you.

Whenever someone disrespects her or directs derogatory comments towards her, she immediately threatens to fight the person. She does this but says that they usually do not end up fighting. It is a way to try to prove herself and eliminate conflict without actually fighting because it rarely causes a physical altercation. It was reported by Danielle that when girls do meet up, there are mostly verbal arguments that end by someone breaking them up before it gets physical. She says that she would fight them, but most of the arguments are not with people that she actually knows. It also is a way for her to develop a tough image. She uses an invitation to fight as a defense mechanism. She does not want others to see that she may really be scared because being popular is important to her.

Jane, who admittedly has been in at least one fight due to FB, describes a particular verbal altercation that occurred because another female stated that she did not like her.

I guess they don't like me so… Like I was mad, I was ready to fight. I was shocked at first cause that person said it and then that's when I got mad. And started talking about it and then started talking about wanting to beat them up and … The person like kind of chickened out when I saw her in person.

Jane proclaims that it was necessary to invite another girl to fight because the girl openly declared that she did not like her. Additionally, Jane shared that she showed the comments to others so they could witness her response and ramp up the conflict. She tried to elevate her status by threatening to beat someone else up. When she saw the other participant in person, the person backed down, and she felt like she was in control and dominant.

Kate, who closed her FB account because she feels that it helps perpetuate unnecessary drama, states that she witnessed a situation where females invited each other to fight, but it became comical due to the numerous invitations without any follow through.

You should go do something right now. No, I'll wait until after school, stuff like that, but it never actually escalated to a physical fight. They just kept making plans and postponing them, and making more plans.

Earlier, it was stated that Danielle always invited girls to fight whenever they challenged her. Later in her interview, though, she shared a real world story about conflict that did not result in physical altercation.

Because of this girl, well we was doing a project and she didn't want to do the project my way and so I had to tell her like you're doing this wrong, you're doing this wrong, she got mad at me and called me all types of negative names. So I got mad and I started calling her all types of names and stuff and before the physical issue came in I just left out of the room and walked away.

She stated that she often threatens to fight, especially behind the computer screen; but, when confronted in person, she decided to walk away. An analysis of Danielle's data concludes that she wants it to appear strong to the public in order to maintain her power, and conserve her social status.

WHO BARKS THE LOUDEST: CONFLICT RESOLUTION STRATEGY

The fourth theme, "Who Barks the Loudest: Conflict Resolution Strategy," is comparable to a small canine who barks ferociously, in order to intimidate a larger canine. The smaller canine hopes to scare the larger canine, but, ultimately, it understands that a physical altercation with the larger canine is unwise. The smaller canine has devised a strategy to appear dominant. This image, derived from the research, is developed in response to the participants' perceived need to save face and maintain respect and social status among their peers. This theme captured how participants deliberately engaged in verbal altercations as a strategy to avoid physical fights. Thus, the louder the public conflict, the greater the likelihood that friends and adults will intervene before a physical altercation can ensue. This final theme also captured various strategies that the participants employed in order to avoid online conflict, which prevented face-face conflict, allowing participants to maintain social status online and in school.

The participants reported the development of strategies and utilization of different techniques to resolve and eliminate conflict online and in the real world. Throughout this study, it became evident that, while the majority of the participants do not want to be involved in physical confrontations, they were not going to back down from one either. However, the arguments that occur are often described by participants as a contest to see who can be the loudest or say the most piercing insult. The participants reported the development of necessary survival techniques in order to maintain their self-respect and social status in the face of being challenged, ostracized, and bullied online and in the real world.

Alisha, who uses Mbuzzy instead of FB now, because she wants to avoid conflict, discusses a real world situation when a girl verbally lashed out at her. Alisha reacted in a manner that displayed she was not going to back down, aware that the security guard was two feet behind the other female and was not going to allow them to fight.

Because she said something to me when I walked by like what the fuck you lookin' at, I'm like, don't get mad at me cause you got beat up. We got into an argument, words was exchanged then I was removed from the situation by one of the school security guards.

In most cases, as indicated by the participants, physical fights are not likely to occur and are replaced with face-to-face verbal arguments in a public place, such as a school hallway. The fact that it is done in a public place is a strategic move by the participants to loudly demonstrate their prowess and simultaneously ask for adult intervention. The adults have the ability to prevent an altercation without damaging the participant's reputation. What the participants want, instead, is to appear that they are not soft, or weak. They want to show the audience that they have street credibility, and they are not to be bothered. Many of the girls have indicated that, if they lose their respect, then everyone will walk on them. If they get walked on, they will not just be fighting one battle, but they will have to fight every day.

Only one out of ten interviewees shared that she had a physical altercation with another female on school grounds due to an Internet conflict. Kiesha describes how she really wished someone would have stopped it from occurring.

No because somewhere in the middle we always kind of like, it's not resolved but it's like interfered with, somebody always jumps in to stop it so it don't escalate. From friends, or teachers, or like whoever is close enough to you to like get in the middle of it, well except for that one time across the street from school. Nobody was able to like interfere with that one so it just escalated all the way to the fight.

Kiesha and the other participants developed a sense of security around having conflict in a school. It was stated that no one was able to interfere, revealing a sense of disappointment that a fight actually occurred. The participants created the illusion that they are not afraid to fight, but, in actuality, the students have developed a hidden set of conflict resolution skills, which have emerged from the perceived need to maintain respectful relationships in an urban neighborhood.

Kate, who self-reports that she does not have a lot of online conflict due to keeping her social network extremely small, describes an occasion where she got into a conflict in school which started online. A security guard, as she reported, ultimately intervened.

Yeah, we were going to fight, in the hallway. We were going to fight each other. She's like I hate B's like you, I'm about to do this and that, I was like okay you're talking, you know, you see in the Facebook where I have to wait like two seconds for you to reply, let's do this right now, I mean come on. Oh the security guard came and broke us up, nothing ever happened, come on.

The participants made sure that they argued in school, in high traffic places, enabling a school security guard to intervene before a fight could ensue. Kate describes another situation that did not involve online conflict, but an argument that began because a girl pointed at her in the lunchroom and proceeded to walk up behind Kate.

I got defensive so I lifted my hand because I was going to punch her in the face and then security guard came over and then I shoved the security guard over and then I picked up my tray and I was about to hit her with it, and somebody grabbed me and I got slammed and she got slammed and we just got carried out.

Kate described the lunchroom as a place with approximately 400 students, one security guard, and two administrators. If Kate or the other girl really wanted to fight, there was a lot of space and opportunity, with little supervision. The girls did not want to fight; they wanted to provide the appearance that they were not afraid to fight. Ultimately, Kate states that the situation was resolved after mediation. Jane, who reports to being in fights at school, but rarely due to FB, discusses a situation that almost caused a fight, in which mediation helped the participants reach a peaceful resolution.

Somebody tried to punk my sister and then I know sometime my sisters don't stick up for themselves so I step in and I show my sister, and I show people that I can stick up for them and I'm not scared of anybody. I bullied them back so they would leave her alone. It almost led to a fight, but then it kind of just went away, because someone stepped in. We had to talk about it in mediation.

Ashley, who self-reported that she desires a lot of FB friends and popularity, but is quick to challenge someone to fight if she feels disrespected, alluded to a situation that was resolved by an intervention from adults where a mediation occurred.

Both of our parents came in and we all sat down in a room together and talked and got the situation basically to a cool level. Yeah. Now, me and her are friends, we talk all the time and stuff like that.

Mediation helped the girls to get over their differences and to become friends. Ashley claimed to have a very bad attitude but did not like getting in trouble at school. She decided to mediate in order to eliminate the conflict. The majority of the participants described successful peaceful outcomes without the loss of respect or social status.

Ignoring conflict was a popular strategy among the female participants in this study. The term "ignoring" was a code that was derived from the research, which presented itself in several different forms. Ignoring was often used as a term that means deleting negative comments without a response, blocking and deleting someone from your FB page, or, in a traditional sense, refraining from a response in a situation where insults or threats have occurred. Harriet reports that she has never been in an argument at school due to FB because she employs the ignoring strategy.

> *No, I haven't a conflict, like I haven't had a conflict on Facebook or any network myself, maybe you know, it's from me seeing conflicts other people have and like it makes me really think like do I really want this person as my friend, cause what if it happens to me. I avoid it by deleting them, blocking them.*

Harriet does not respond to conflict, as she noted what happens to others who do. Instead, she elects to delete the person of conflict and block them from her page. This strategy eliminates the conflict, eliminating the possibility of a physical altercation. She states that she is not the type of person who likes to argue and that she tries to avoid conflict.

Charmaine also describes herself as someone who wants to be liked and, conversely, will try to avoid conflict by refraining from engaging in one. She states, "I didn't react to it; I just deleted her off my page and went on with it." Additionally, she was the lone participant that stated that it did not matter if she got embarrassed online. "If I feel embarrassed or punked, well I just got to feel embarrassed or punked or whatever." Charmaine indicated that she feels different about online disrespect because it is just words. Charmaine states that words do not affect her. In person, she confirms that she will try to seek out help if someone is only verbally aggressive toward her. Ashley agreed with Charmaine in regards to the importance of ignoring online conflict. Ashley takes it a step further and discusses how she vents to her mother and asks for advice when consistent Internet conflict arises.

> *Yeah a lot of people make negative comments but I don't pay it no attention. If I get frustrated by it, I really just either talk to my mom or somebody, or one of my sisters about the situation and they be just like just let it go, if they're not trying to throw their hands at you or like you didn't see them and they didn't swing on you, just let it go, they're not going to touch you so, this is a computer we're talking about.*

Ashley was able to provide an example of how she was able to let online conflict go, without a response. Ashley used an adult figure as a resource for venting her frustrations instead of reacting and creating more conflict. The varying uses of the ignoring strategy employed by the participants illuminate the importance of letting online conflict dissolve by not reacting in a manner that creates more conflict.

Several participants mentioned another method for resolving or avoiding conflict, which involved effectively communicating with the opposition in a private forum without an audience. The participants who indicated this strategy as an option explained that a private conversation eliminated the possibility of embarrassment, decreasing the risk of losing respect and social status. Kiesha describes the difference between how she feels when disrespected online, in front of a public, virtual audience, versus during a private phone conversation.

Then when I feel disrespected and I feel the need to disrespect them back, I don't feel the need to like bite my tongue and not say nothing or say oh you hurt my feelings. I'm going to disrespect you the same way you disrespected me. Yes, I can see if we were like talking on the phone and you were saying that stuff to me, nobody else can hear it or can't see it, but for other people to see it is like embarrassing, it's like embarrassing me.

 If it were a private space, the arguments might not have festered. However, as soon as it became public, it created a larger conflict, drawing online and in-person crowds. Kiesha demonstrates that the public nature of Internet conflict escalates quickly because it is in front of her friends, which causes an embarrassing situation. Upon being disrespected and embarrassed in a social setting, Kiesha feels the need to respond in a way that will save face and earn social capital by retaliating verbally. If the argument was a private one, she admits that the conflict will be a lot less important and less damaging to her reputation. Harriet discusses how she feels about online conflict and states how she would much rather have a face to face conversation.

Because on the Internet stuff gets blown out of proportion like that person could have said something back to me that, you know, could have just started a whole other thing and I just didn't want that so I would rather see the person face-to-face.

She does not like to respond to conflict online because she feels that miscommunication can, too often, cause misunderstandings.

Many of the participants' online misunderstandings may be reduced by choosing not to respond to conflict, or by responding in a mature way, during a private conversation. Harriet goes on to describe a situation that could have easily ended up in a serious conflict, but did not, because both parties decided to have a mature, private, online conversation. The conversation was conducted through inbox messaging, which is not for public view.

Like my boyfriend, well my ex-boyfriend Terry like we just recently broke up. I was with him for like three years and then he cheated on me and had a baby by another female. I found out because she added me on Facebook and then like she's seen pictures of me and him together and then she asked me about it and I said yeah, and then she sent me a picture of those three at the hospital. No it didn't cause a conflict between me and her; we were both old enough to talk about it privately. No, we weren't disrespectful.

The boyfriend was cheating and communicating on FB with both girls. However, the two girls communicated on FB, and he was caught cheating. FB helped them resolve a conflict because they both handled it maturely. Both females were respectful of one another, spoke in private, and, as a result, the conflict did not escalate. It appears that most conflicts can be resolved if the participants attempt to communicate about the conflicts that are occurring. Some participants were able to communicate with the opposition on their own and others demonstrated that they needed the help of adults acting as mediators. Regardless, the majority of participants reported that they were able to resolve conflicts by effectively communicating or attempting to refrain from negative responses, preventing embarrassment within the public forum.

CHAPTER SUMMARY

The four themes discussed in this chapter were: FB Thuggin, Moving Too Fast, You Gonna Have to See Me, and Who Barks the Loudest. All four themes were relevant to the experiences of urban adolescent Black females who participated in this qualitative study on cyberbullying.

Many of the participants use Facebook to elevate their social status, by presenting themselves as the bully to prevent being bullied. Additionally, many of them measure their social status by the number of FB friends they have. The participants alleged that the relationships formed online lacked substance because they were formed too quickly and without establishing any form of true friendship. Often, the participants described how FB friends often become online bullies, because there is no true loyalty, or bond, among FB friends. When cyberbullying arose among the participants and created conflict, a similar strategy was utilized by almost every participant. Many of the participants engaged in conflict to save face, to prevent the appearance of being weak, and to mitigate the loss of respect as social capital.

Even though many of the participants were able to provide detailed descriptions of conflicts that occurred, all of the participants were also able to discuss several strategies used to avoid, reduce, and resolve conflict. The following and final chapter of this study will provide further summary of the findings while also describing the implications for recommendation and the study's limitations.

CHAPTER 5

DISCUSSION

Chapter 5 includes study implications guided by the research questions. The research questions are: How do urban Black adolescent females describe their experiences as participants and victims of cyberbullying. If they were victimized, what were the outcomes of being cyberbullied? This question is important because, aside from this study, cyberbullying in an urban high school environment, with a specific focus on Black adolescent females, is essentially un-researched (Li, 2005; Lenhart, Madden, & Hitlin, 2005; Li, 2006; Hinduja & Patchin, 2007).

Additionally, this chapter will address the study's limitations, and recommendations will be made based on the implications, in order to assist educators with teaching Black females how to deal effectively with conflict off and online, without sacrificing social status and/or the perception of respect. Currently, cyberbullying research focuses heavily on quantifying incidents of cyberbullying. This research provides a qualitative snapshot of cyberbullying as a phenomenon and its effect on a specific population, which, congruently, reports limited discourse within the scholarly literature (Hinduja & Patchin, 2008). This study focused on specific, intimate experiences shared by a select group of urban adolescent Black females.

IMPLICATIONS OF FINDINGS

The findings of this research were derived from the development of four themes. The four themes originated from the participants' identity, relationships, conflicts, and conflict resolution. Current cyberbullying research indicates that cyberbullying has the potential to distress adolescents at school, affecting their identity development (Ybarra et al., 2007). Females, especially, are affected in this way, as they spend more time online than their male peers and because they are quicker to form significant social relationships on-line (Juvonen & Gross, 2008). However, the literature does not unearth how cyberbullying affects populations in an urban school environment, specifically adolescent Black females (Wollack & Mitchell, 2000; Li, 2006; Lenhart, Madden, Macgill, & Smith, 2007). The implication interwoven into each of the study's four themes was the importance of maintaining respect and social status at all times in order to save face and mitigate the threat of being bullied.

Respect and social status. Respect and social status are essential to this study's participants, as constructing a liked, or even feared, social image places these girls, in their minds, at the top of a hierarchy designed to conserve their safety in their school, neighborhoods, and online spaces. When relational aggression, in this case as cyberbullying, occurs among urban Black youth, little effort is exerted to examine how or why it manifests in social contexts or how it may distress Black youth (Herrenkohl et al., 2001). This research studied and analyzed a group of Black females' experiences with cyberbullying. The data from the interviews confirms that cyberbullying can negatively impact the participants' social status and the level of respect they receive from their peers within their school and community, specifically when the girls do not respond with the requisite aggression.

The research supports the notion offered by the participants of this study. For example, prior research asserts that Black youth may respond aggressively in a social setting if acts of relational aggression occur because respect must be maintained to uphold one's social status (Yager & Rotheram-Borus, 2000). The participants in this study concurred that they were inclined to fight to protect their social status if they felt that they had been disrespected publicly. Often, the participants were willing to fight, in spite of their preference for peaceful resolution, because such conflict was thought to be the only way to preserve their social acceptance. These girls portrayed a willingness in order to maintain their respect and to ensure that they were not viewed as weak. The participants shared that the perception of frailty, within the urban community, is preyed upon, potentially leading to varying degrees of continuous harassment. According to Deutsch and Jones (2008), many urban, Black youth are ingrained with a distorted and magnified perception of respect that becomes a micro-system of their socialization. The females within this study reported that they learned from an early age that losing the respect of one's friends translates to being walked on and pushed over. Accordingly, they all shared their own strategies for dealing with conflict without being victimized.

Bullying, cyberbullying, and victimization in an urban environment. Conversely, none of the participants reported feeling like a bully or feeling victimized, offering, instead, that their reactions to confrontation were aimed at preventing such feelings. Bullying usually occurs when an individual or a small group of individuals want to exercise their dominance (power) over another individual (McQuade, Colt, & Meyer, 2009). At times, they, admittedly, exhibited characteristics of both the bully and the victim. The girls in this study have developed a defense strategy, a mental mechanism employed on and offline in order to maintain their individual social status and popularity. These girls possess a unique ability to instantly adapt to any situation in order to maintain their respect and social status.

Cyberbullying, a more cerebral form of traditional bullying, employs quick wit, cleverness, and computer proficiency (Patchin & Hinduja 2007), which the participants acquired over much time spent online. For example, they often use the Internet and "FB Thuggin" to create an idealized version of their image with a focus on appearing tough, yet social. Bullies are defined as someone who repeatedly attacks another individual psychologically, physically, or verbally, usually because the other individual is weaker in size, strength, or even social status (Olweus, 1993). Often, the bullying that occurred among the participants was a verbal attack on someone who was in their social network of friends. The attacks were described as retaliation on a form of disrespect. Rarely, did the participants describe a scenario where they initiated conflict, representing themselves as a bully.

Most of the participants did not directly admit to employing "FB Thuggin," a form of cyberbullying, but they often described how others participated in it. It appeared that the participants were aware of how it occurred, but not willing to own their involvement. In many instances, the participants admitted to providing a harsh response to a hurtful comment, which, ultimately, created a war of derogatory insults until it inevitably escalated to an invitation to a fight. This resulting conflict is a common by-product of "FB Thuggin," a strategy used to prove one's toughness to other online viewers. A teen's social self is often created by what he or she thinks others see, which has the potential to affect what others think, as well (Rice & Dolgin 2008).

As middle and high school age females develop, their desire to "fit in" with certain groups in school becomes part of their internal journey (Dellasega & Nixon, 2003). Girls try to "fit in" online to meet the expectations of their peers, paying particular attention to acquiring the correct identity, social networking page, and netspeak vocabulary (McQuade et al., 2009). These participants advise that increased popularity, and the subsequent elevation in social status, can severely diminish, even eliminate, instances of bullying. Therefore, "FB Thuggin" represents, for these girls, a method for developing an "Ideal Self", controlling how they are perceived online and, by extension, in person.

Relational aggression and online relationship development. This current study mirrors the results of other similar research regarding the frequency with which relational aggressive tactics are occurring online. The lack of true online friendships often opened the door for relational aggression to occur among the female participants and their online friends (Espelage et al., 2003; Nansel et al., 2001). According to Underwood (2003), girls manifest their aggression indirectly, by adopting socially and relationally aggressive techniques. For example, a girl might exemplify such aggression by spreading a rumor on the Internet about another girl. The participants in this study frequently depicted experiences where conflicts began due to rumors, gossip, and direct insults. When these types of tactics were perceived, the participants responded by developing a strategy for protecting their respect and social status.

The participants in this study suggest that such victimization occurs because friendships formed online develop without the otherwise prerequisite establishment of trust. Often, in the online realm, a person is referred to as a friend simply because a friend request is made and accepted. According to Li (2006), 50 percent of cyberbullying victims know the perpetrators. This statistic calls attention to the fact that half of cyberbullies are friends of their victims.

The study's participants also indicate that online relationships form more quickly because online users paint an embellished picture of themselves, which can be intriguing and equally dishonest. Such dishonesty can ruin relationships and prevent true friendships from forming. Formerly, high school was the preferred venue for creating and destroying relationships. McClung (2006) advises that girls experience high school as a breeding ground for broken relationships due to pressure from large populations, boys, self-imposed, identity issues.

As a result of technology, these same pressures are experienced online because school age children often form large networks of online friends without first establishing true relationships. The online world has joined the classroom and school halls as a new social breeding ground for relational aggression, a disguised and manipulative aggression, which is designed to affect another person's social status and relationships (Xie, Farmer, & Cairns, 2003). The participants in this study used relational aggressive tactics similarly to participants in other national research (Underwood, 2003), but, conversely, this study showed what occurred among a population of Black females after the aggressive tactics reached a point of end. When relational aggression achieved its boiling point, a cycle of conflict began.

Cycle of conflict. When the participants invited another individual to fight, they used the term "Now You Gonna Have to See Me." This kind of escalation occurs when a conflict reaches a verbal boiling point, causing the users to feel that something drastic must be done to save face and re-establish respect. Prior research establishes an understanding of traditional cyberbullying, arguing that its effects do not transcend the online boundaries rarely progressing to face to face conflict (Ybarra & Mitchell, 2004). Even though the results of this research support this finding, the participants suggest that additional steps must be taken to terminate the conflict without the loss of respect and social status, specifically in urban communities.

The participants describe how most conflicts that began online and escalated to an invitation to fight, usually unfold in a public, real-world location, such as school. Unspoken, but exposed through the described experiences, the participants purposely follow up on their threats in a public place, such as a crowded school hallway, where both participants loudly present themselves as unafraid. Most commonly, the arguing increases in volume until an adult is made aware and intervenes accordingly.

This strategy is a calculated risk because it could result in a physical altercation. However, the data from this study indicates that the risk is worth taking because the majority of situations reported, ended without physical violence. The desired outcome is that no one fights, nor loses any respect or social status. According to Anderson (1999), respect is viewed as social capital, which is highly valued because other forms of capital may be obsolete and, as such, not valued. The participants divulged that the appearance of a willingness to fight was usually sufficient to squelch the social peer pressure.

The embarrassment of public humiliation in an urban social setting has lent this study's participants to develop a cycle of strategies for conflict resolution. Gonick (2004) characterizes adolescence as a time when young women feel they can only count on themselves and when any vulnerability can provoke social anxieties about the world in which they must survive. Online embarrassment creates social anxieties, which, ultimately, caused conflict for most of the participants in this study. The aforementioned cycle was described by the participants as a conflict of words that would continue back and forth, each time the participants would attempt to embarrass the opposition more than they were embarrassed previously. Finally, an invitation to fight occurred, followed by a public show of verbal aggression, which, the participants hoped would be halted by adult intervention.

Winning respect in this manner has a way of delivering a message to others that the victor will now be free from persecution and granted safe passage at school and in their neighborhood (Jones, 2004). The loud commotion in a public place serves to deliver the message. However, the altercation typically gets interrupted by an adult in close proximity, giving the impression that, if unimpeded, the two individuals would become violent. Once the adult intervenes, they assume the burden of resolving to conflict. Once the adult facilitates peaceful resolution, the participants indicated that the conflict usually dissipates without the loss of social status or respect. The value of respect in the urban community is pertinent and important to the implications of this research, as illustrated in the "Cycle of Conflict."

FIGURE 5.1.

CYCLE OF CONFLICT

Verbal Disrespect

Retaliation /Save Face

Embarassment Causing A Completion of Verbal Argument

You Gonna Have To See Me

Public Display of Verbal Agression

Adult Intervention Before A Physical Altercation Ensues

Mediation/Peaceful Resolution

Safety Conserved

Respect and Social Status Maintained

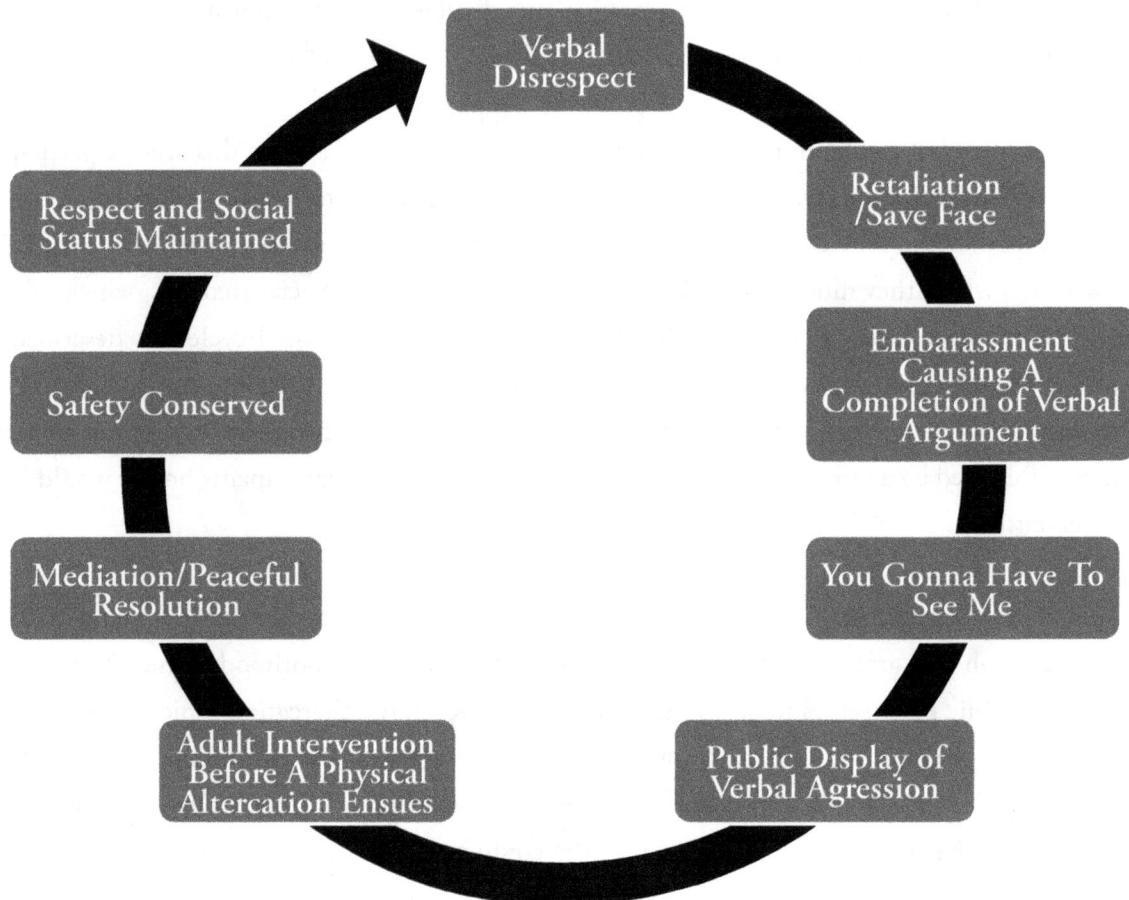

Implication for research on black adolescent females. Research on Black girls often stereotypes and generalizes their behavior. Black girls are often positioned as loud and aggressive, or limitedly researched within scholarly literature (Fordham, 1993). Yager and Rotheram-Borus (2000), suggest that Black youth may respond more aggressively than other cultural groups would in a social setting. The findings from this study are in disagreement. The participants in this study did not react differently than other cultural groups massively studied within the cyberbullying research. According to Ybarra and Mitchell (2004), cyberbullying is anonymous, can happen anywhere at any time, but it usually does not lead to face to face altercations. This study composed of Black females concurs with the national research on cyberbullying.

The participants in this study did not demonstrate loud and aggressive behavior. Overwhelmingly the participants shared that they did not like conflict, nor would they purposely attempt to bully anyone. Unanimously, the participants agreed that an action from a perpetrator required a response, the aggressiveness of which was based on the level of disrespect conveyed in the offense. While some of them invoked a higher tolerance for insulting behavior, eight of the ten participants reported that they needed to "save face" in all situations. The other two advised that they would only attempt to "save face" if they were physically attacked. According to the research on urban Blacks, respect may be re-established by fighting and winning the physical altercation; another way is for the individual to present themselves as verbally tougher (Anderson 1999; Jones, 2004; Miller, 2008). The majority of the participants preferred to "save face" by presenting themselves as verbally tougher when they are verbally accosted online or in a real world setting.

Among urban Black females, a need to save face in public places like school, or even over the Internet, was denoted as important by the participants in this study. The importance of saving face in the midst of adversity was not to look for attention, but, rather, to maintain social status among peers and reduce the potential of being bullied. Miller (2008) describes disrespect among urban Black females as a possible safety hazard. The loss of social status creates an opportunity to be preyed upon, because of the negative perception of being weak (Anderson, 1999). The participants reported a desire to peacefully resolve most situations and often looked to adults for assistance and intervention.

LIMITATIONS

This study's researcher was not able to gain access to the actual Facebook pages of the participants, due to Internal Review Board (IRB) limitations. Access to Facebook pages would have allowed the researcher to function as an observer. A second limitation of this study was that it was conducted at only one high school situated in an urban environment. This particular design was intentional, but conducting such research in various locations could undoubtedly lend additional, valuable insight into the studied population's experiences with cyberbullying. In the future, a diverse pool of adolescent research candidates, from various urban high schools could increase the range of reported experiences and subsequent coping strategies. Future opportunities for research could extend this study to urban Black adolescent females across the nation.

RECOMMENDATIONS

This study will provide two primary sets of recommendations, both aimed at helping educators with effective conflict resolution between adolescent urban Black females. The initial recommendations will be suggestions for educators, in which tools will be provided to teach urban adolescent Black females how to reduce online conflict while maintaining respectful relationships. The second set of recommendations will assist educators in the development of their ability to intervene in such situations, without diminishing the respect or social status of the participants.

RECOMMENDATIONS FOR GIRLS

The first recommendation for urban educators is to teach Black adolescent females the importance of maintaining intimate social networks, as smaller networks can provide lower opportunity for conflict. Intimate networks can be maintained by suggesting that FB pages remain private. Additionally, explaining to the students that having 800 friends while professing a desire for privacy is fallacy and unrealistic, as intimate life details are often shared without the formation of truly devoted relationships. Throughout this study, several of the participants stated that their Facebook page was private, but they had large amounts of friends, and they frequently experienced online conflict. The participants who limited their network to close real world friends and family experienced minimal conflict. Those particular participants were able to use Facebook as a tool to enhance their social relationships without consistently worrying about maintaining their images. The participants stated that their real world friends and family know who they really are; there was no need to change their identity while online.

It may be too late to suggest an intimate network because, according to research, teens regularly use the Internet from six to nine hours a day (Berson & Ferron, 2002). This study, concurring with national research, reports an average of six hours a day was spent online among the ten participants. Most teens spend an extreme amount of time online, actively cultivating large social networks. After explaining the importance of intimate networks, students should be encouraged to take the time to delete individuals from their account who are not their real world friends. The elimination of FB friends with no real world connection will reduce fake friends, inspiring a more trustful, intimate network in which personal business can be shared, without worry of fake friends misusing the shared information in order to cause harm.

According to the results of this research, it is easier to walk away from conflict before it escalates to physical violence. Educators should teach their students that it is acceptable to walk away from conflict (Shakoor & Chalmers, 1986). Walking away after the initial incident can contain the problem without impacting social status. At times, a conflict may involve a real world friend and has the potential to become viral, as well. If the arguments become viral, emphasize the importance of blocking that real world friend's access to their online account (McQuade et al., 2009). Often, when the participants from this study blocked and deleted anyone who created conflict for them, the conflict ended up dissolving on its own. The fuel of a sharp-witted response fueled conflict until it elevated and a need to save face evinced itself. The research revealed that most friendships could be salvaged through mediation if the cyber arguments did not spiral out of control.

Additionally, educators should stress the importance of why students should maintain their real world identity (Thomas, 2007). Creating a false identity, or "FB Thuggin", will often catch up to the students and create conflict. Often, students use the phrase "keeping it 100", which is a popular contemporary synonym for being true to oneself and always behaving as a "real" person. Students should be reminded of their creed and encouraged to exude self-respect. For students who participate in "FB Thuggin" and develop unrealistically tough personas, this research shows an elevated potential for consistent challenges to their social status. If students are urged to maintain their true identity among intimate networks, trustful online relationships can flourish (Rosen, 2006).

Educators can ask students if they would be willing to share intimate details of their lives on the morning announcements at school and then place them on the bulletin board in the cafeteria. Students may not be willing to do so, so educators should challenge their logic, asking them why they are willing to do so online. This has the potential to create teachable moments in which the educator can provide a few additional reminders on Internet etiquette.

Basic Internet etiquette that derived from this study includes staying out of online conversations that do not pertain to the individual in question (Burgess-Proctor, Patchin, & Hinduja, 2009). The insertion of an opinion online often created conflict for the participants in this study. It was proclaimed that inserting themselves into others conversations led to misunderstandings that, ultimately, led to potential conflict.

Secondly, if a misunderstanding occurs online, this study showed that trying to work out the disagreement online, could lead to additional misunderstandings, especially if not done privately. Additionally, ignoring inflammatory comments that don't solicit a specific response can reduce the perpetuation of the cycle of conflict (Sunburst Visual Media, 2003). The most successful participants in this study, in regards to resolving conflict, did so by having mature, private, face-to-face conversations. Lastly, teachers should advise the students that, if a conflict has to be resolved online, it should be done privately, by messaging the individual (Lenhart et al., 2007). The more public the feud is; the more likely one of the participants will develop a need to "save face".

RECOMMENDATIONS FOR EDUCATORS PRACTICE

As an urban educator, the major implication from this research, which will assist pedagogy, is to understand the importance of respect within the urban community, specifically among Black females. Simply put, understanding the origins of respect is not enough; it must also be applied to situations, by being cognizant of how it influenced the decisions of the participants involved (Bennet-Johnson, 2004). Self respect should be modeled as an important and necessary aspect of respect. Respect needs to be internalized instead of solely sought externally (Richard, Deci, & Edward, 2000). While many of the participants from this study placed an emphasis on their perceptions of how other people treated them and valued their worth, only two participants discussed the importance of respecting themselves.

Educators can help the girls "save face" by absorbing the conflict and getting involved early before it escalates (Sunburst Visual Media, 2003). The results from the analysis of this data showed that mediation between two conflicting parties is effective. The adult mediator should offer the mediation as a viable alternative, make it mandatory, be objective, and work towards peaceful outcomes (Tolson, McDonald, & Moriarty, 1990). The results of this study showed that if students develop an understanding of the educator's policy, it will become an accepted practice and neither party will lose respect because it appears that the school mandated the resolution.

One technique that can be applied is to create a contract/agreement for the girls to sign upon completion of the mediation. The mediation agreement can let all students know the consequences of breaking a mediation agreement (Burell, Zirbel, & Allen, 2003). The consequences must be something that is certainly enforceable. The educator must remain consistent and keep the students accountable if agreements are broken, making a disciplinary example of someone, in order to demonstrate to the majority of students just how serious the agreements must be taken. The data from this study revealed that, when students mediated, conflict was often resolved, and students confessed to not wanting to be suspended or arrested for fighting. Additionally, a skilled mediator can teach and encourage girls to have appropriate face-to-face conversations in order to resolve conflict, further teaching them that, instead of confronting someone in order to win respect, they should seek and gain respect by pursuing a mature and peaceful outcome (Tolson et al., 1990).

CONCLUSION

This study has provided a snapshot of how cyberbullying was experienced among a specific group of Black females, which may lend a voice to the otherwise overlooked experiences of other Black females. Previously, limited discourse has been provided regarding urban adolescent Black females and their experiences with cyberbullying (Epstein & Kazmierczack, 2007). The formation of this study materialized due to an overwhelming amount of conflict that the researcher witnessed in his role as a high school administrator. Often, the conflicts involved urban adolescent Black females.

Many of the conflicts originated on the Internet and materialized at high school the following day, disrupting the educational environment. Initially, the researcher believed that Internet conflict, specifically within the urban environment, most frequently led to physical altercations. Upon completion of the research, it was actualized that physical fights are not as prominent as once generalized. More importantly, the results promulgated a chain of events that occurred, almost invariably, each time a conflict arose between the participants. Understanding the linkage and where to enter the conflict, as an educator, provides value and an additional piece to the puzzle needed to minimize conflict between urban adolescent Black females, without jeopardizing their social status and the related sense of respect.

REFERENCES

Adler, F. (1975). *Sisters in crime: The rise of the new female criminal.* New York: McGraw-Hill.

Anderson, E. (1999). *Code of the streets.* New York: W.W Norton and Company.

Astor, R., & Meyer, H. (2009). School violence and theoretically atypical schools: The Principal's centrality in orchestrating safe schools. *American Education Research Journal, 46,* 423-461.

Astor, R., Benbenishty, R., & Estrada, J. (2009). School violence and theoretically atypical schools: The Principals centrality in orchestrating safe schools. *American Education Research Journal, 46*(2), 423-461.

Baldry, C. A. (2004). The impact of direct and indirect bullying on the mental and physical health of Italian youngsters. *Aggressive Behavior, 30,* 343-355.

Baltes, P. B., & Shaie, W. (1973). *Life-span developmental psychology: Personality and socialization.* New York: Academic Press.

Beane, A. L. (1999). *The bully free classroom: Over 100 tips and strategies for Teachers K-8.* Minneapolis, MN: Free Spirit Publishing Inc.

Beasley, B. (2004). *What is cyberbullying?.* Retrieved February 3, 2010, from www.cyberbullying.org

Benbenishty, R., & Astor, R. A. (2005). *School violence in context: Culture, neighborhood, family, school, and gender.* New York: Oxford University Press.

Bennet-Johnson, E. (2004). The Root of School Violence: Cause and recommendations for a plan of action. *College Student Journal, 38*(2), 199-202.

Berson, R. I., Berson, J. M., & Ferron, M. J. (2002). Emerging risks of violence in the digital age: Lessons for educators from an online study of adolescent girls in the United States. *Journal of School Violence, 1,* 51-71.

Bronfenbrenner, U. (1979). *The ecology of human development: Experiments by nature and design.* Cambridge, MA: Harvard University Press.

Brown, M. L., & Gilligan, C. (1992). *Meeting at the crossroads: Women's psychology and girls' development.* New York: Ballantine Books.

Bullen, P., & Harre, N. (2000). *The Internet: Its effect on safety and behavior: Implications for adolescents.* Retrieved September 4, 2010, from http://www.netsafe.org.nz/research/research_safety.aspx

Burell, N. A., Zirbel, C. S., & Allen, M. (2003). Evaluating peer mediation outcomes in educational settings: A meta-analytic review. *Conflict Resolution Quarterly, 21,* 7-26.

Burgess-Proctor, A., Patchin, J., & Hinduja, S. (2009). Cyberbullying and online harassment: Reconceptualizing the victimization of adolescent girls. In *Female crime victims: Reality reconsidered* (pp. 162-176). Upper Saddle River, NY: Prentice Hall.

Butterfield, L., & Broad, H. (2002). *Children, young people and the Internet.* Retrieved November 17, 2010, from http://www.netsafe.org.nz/articles/articleschildren.aspx

Cairns, R. B., Cairns, B. D., Neckerman, H. J., Ferguson, L. L., & Gariepy, J. L. (1989). Growth and aggression: Childhood to early adolescence. *Developmental Psychology, 25,* 320-330.

Calvert, S. (2002). *Identity construction on the Internet.* Westport, CT: Greenwood Publishing Group.

Caravan (2006). *Cyber-Bully-Pre-Teen.* Retrieved March 23, 2010, from http://www.fightcrime.org/cyberbullying/cyberbullyingpreteen.pdf

Center for Safe and Responsible Internet Use (n.d.). . Retrieved February 23, 2010, from http://csriu.org/cyberbullying/newsreports.html

Chen, G. (2008). Communities, students, schools, and school crime. *Urban Education, 43,* 301-316.

Chestang, L. (1976). *Environmental influences on social functioning the Black experience in the diverse society: Implications for social policy.* New York: Association Press.

Chu, J. (2005). You wanna take this online?. *Time, 166,* 52-55.

Clark, R. D., & Lab, S. P. (2000). Community characteristics and in school criminal victimization. *Journal of Criminal Justice, 28*, 33-42.

Colt, J. (2009). *Building-level school administrators' perceptions of cyberbullying among students under their supervision: Implications for prevention and intervention.* Unpublished doctoral dissertation, St. John Fisher College, Rochester, New York.

Cottrell, R. R., & McKenzie, J. F. (2005). *Health promotion and education research methods: Using the five-chapter thesis/dissertation model.* Sudbury, Massachusetts: Jones and Bartlett Publishers.

Creswell, J. W. (2003). *Research design: qualitative, quantitative, and mixed methods approaches.* California: Sage Publications, Inc.

Daly, K. (1989). Gender and varieties of white-collar crime. *Criminology, 27*, 769-764.

Davies, J. C. (1970). Violence and aggression: Innate or not?. *The Western Political Quarterly, 23*, 611-623.

Dellasega, C., & Nixon, C. (2003). *Girl wars: 12 strategies that will end female bullying.* New York: Simon and Schuster.

Deutsch, N. L., & Jones, J. N. (2008). Show me an ounce of respect: Respect and authority in adult-youth relationships in after-school programs. *Journal of Adolescent Research, 26*, 667 688.

Dictionary.com (2010). *Poverty.* Retrieved October 16, 2010, from http://dictionary.reference.com/browse/poverty

Dictionary.com (2011). *Conflict.* Retrieved May 15, 2011, from http://dictionary.reference.com/browse/conflict

Elliot, D. (1994). *Youth violence: An overview.* Retrieved March 3, 2010, from http://www.cde.state.co.us/artemis/ucb6/ucb61092ad719942Internet.pdf

Epstein, A., & Kazmierczack, J. (2007). Cyberbullying: What Teachers, Social workers, and Administrators should know. *Illinois Child Welfare, 3*, 41-51.

Erikson, E. (1968). *Identity youth and crisis.* New York: W. W. Norton and Company.

Espelage, L. D., Holt, K. M., & Henkel, R. R. (2003). Examination of peer group contextual effects on aggressive behavior during early adolescence. *Child Development, 74*, 205-220.

Find Law (2010). *U.S. Supreme Court: PLESSY v. FERGUSON, 163 U.S. 537 (1896)*. Retrieved October 11, 2010, from http://caselaw.lp.findlaw.com/scripts/getcase.pl?court=us&vol=163&invol=537

Flouri, E., & Buchanan, A. (2003). The role of mother involvement and father involvement in adolescent bullying behavior. *Journal of Interpersonal Violence, 18*, 634-644.

Fordham, S. (1993). "Those loud black girls": (Black) Women, silence, and gender "Passing" in the academy. *Anthropology and Education Quarterly, 24*, 3-32.

Gonick, M. (2004). The mean girl crisis: Problematizing representations of girls friendships. *Feminism and Psychology, 14*, 395-400.

Gooden, J. S., & Harrington, S. Y. (2005). The unsafe school choice option: A snapshot. *Planning and Changing, 36*(3 & 4), 133-145.

Gross, E. F. (2004). Adolescent Internet use: What we expect, what teens report. *Applied Developmental Psychology, 25*, 633-649.

Harris, A. R., & Walton, M. D. (2008). Thank you for making me write this letter: Narrative skills and the management of conflict in urban schools. *Urban Rev, 41*, 287-311.

Havighurst, R. J. (1972). *Development task and education* (3rd ed.). New York: David McKay.

Hawker, D. S., & Boulton, M. J. (2000). Twenty years' research on peer victimization and psychosocial maladjustment: A meta-analytic review of cross-sectional studies. *Journal of Child Psychology and Psychiatry, 41*, 441-455.

Hazelden Foundation (2007). *Olweus bullying prevention program research and history*. Retrieved October 16, 2010, from www.olweus.org/public/document/olweus_research_history.pdf

Hemmings, A. (2003). Fighting for respect in urban high schools. *Teachers College Record, 105*, 416-437.

Herrenkohl, T. I., Huang, B., Kosterman, R., Hawkins, J. D., Catalano, R. F., & Smith, B. H. (2001). A comparison of social development leading to violent behavior in late adolescence for childhood initiators and adolescent initiators of violence. *Journal of Research in Crime and Delinquency, 38*, 45-63.

Hinduja, S., & Patchin, J. (2007). Offline consequences of online victimization: School violence and delinquency. *Journal of School Violence, 6*, 89-112.

Hinduja, S., & Patchin, J. (2008). Cyberbullying: An exploratory analysis of factors related to offending and victimization. *Deviant Behavior, 29*, 129-156.

Hinduja, S., & Patchin, J. (2008). Personal information of adolescents on the Internet: A quantitative content analysis of MySpace. *Journal of Adolescence, 31*, 125-146.

Hoover, J., & Oliver, R. (1996). *The bullying prevention handbook: A guide for principals, teachers, and counselors.* Bloomington, IN: National Educational Service.

Jackson, L. A., Zhao, Y., Witt, E. A., Fitzgerald, H. E., & Eye, A. V. (2009). Gender, race and morality in the virtual world and its relationship to morality in the real world. *Springer Science and Business Media,* 859-869.

Johnson, S. B., Frattaroli, S., Wright, J. L., Pearson-Fields, C. B., & Cheng, T. L. (2004). Urban youth perception on violence and the necessity of fighting. *Injury Prevention, 10*, 287-291.

Jones, N. (2004). Girls fight: Negotiating conflict and violence in distressed inner-city neighborhoods. *Dissertations Abstracts International,* 1-237. (UMI No. 3138034)

Juvonen, J., & Gross, E. F. (2008). Extending the school grounds: Bullying experiences in cyberspace. *Journal of School Health, 78*, 496-505.

Kakar, S.. (1997). *Juvenile Violence and Violence in Schools* (). : .

Kowalski, R., & Limber, S. (2007). Electronic bullying among middle school students. *Journal of Adolescents Health, 41*, 22-30.

Kramer, R. (2000). Poverty, inequality, and youth violence. *Annals AAPSS, 567*, 123-139.

Lei, J. L. (2003). (Un)Necessary Toughness?: Those "Loud Black Girls" and "Quiet Asian Boys". *Anthropology and Education Quarterly, 34,* 158-181.

Lenhart, A. (2006). *Presentation: Social networking, safety testimony by Amanda Lenhart, Senior Research Specialist, Pew Internet & American Life Project to the House Committee on Energy and Commerce Subcommittee on Telecommunications and the Internet hearing on H.R. 5319, The Deleting On-line Predators Act of 2006.* Retrieved February 3, 2010, from http://www.pewInternet.org/Presentations/2006/Testimony-by-Amanda-Lenhart-to-the-House-Subcommittee-on-Telecommunications-and-the-Internet.aspx

Lenhart, A. (2007). *Cyberbullying and online teens* [Data file]. Available from Data memo from the Pew Internet & American Life Project: http://www.pewInternet.org/~/media//Files/Reports/2007/PIP%20 Cyberbullying%20Memo.pdf.pdf

Lenhart, A., Madden, M., & Hitlin, P. (2005). *Teens and technology: Youth are leading the transition to a fully wired and mobile nation.* Washington, DC: Pew Internet and American Life Project

Lenhart, A., Madden, M., Macgill, A., & Smith, A. (2007). *Teens and the Social Media* Pew/Internet and American Life Project.

Li, Q. (2005). New bottle but old wine: A research of cyberbullying in schools. *Computers in Human Behavior, 23,* 2-15.

Li, Q. (2006). Cyberbullying in schools: A research of gender differences. *Scholl Psychology International, 27,* 157-170.

Lind-Chesney, M. (1997). *The female offender: Girls, woman, and crime.* Thousand Oaks, Calif: Sage Publications.

Lindle, J. C. (2008). School Safety, Real or Imagined Fear?. *Educational Policy, 22*(1), 28-44.

Lipsman, A. (2006). *Microsoft sites rank as top web property in June, according to comScore World Metrix.* Retrieved November 17, 2010, from http://www.comscore.com.com/press/release.asp?press=976

Lisante, J. E. (2005). *Cyberbullying: No muscles needed.* Retrieved February 9, 2010, from http://www. connectforkids.org/node/3116

Lockwood, D. (1997). *Violence among middle and high school students: Analysis and implications for prevention* (Department of Justice). Washington, DC: National Institute of Justice Research in Brief.

Lombroso, C., & Ferrero, W. (1895). *The female offender.* New York: D. Appleton.

Marshall, C., & Rossman, G. (2011). *Designing qualitative research* (5th ed.). Thousand Oaks, California: Sage Publications Inc.

Mason, K. L. (2008). Cyberbullying: A preliminary assessment for school personnel. *Psychology in the Schools, 45,* 323-349.

McClung, S. R. (2006). Cyberbullying: Mean girls or authentic relationships (Doctoral dissertation, St. Mary's University, 2006). *Dissertations Abstracts International,* 1-167.

McQuade, S. C., Colt, J. P., & Meyer, N. B. (2009). *Cyber Bullying: Protecting kids and adults from online bullies.* Westport, Connecticut: Praeger.

McQuade, S., & Sampat, N. (2008, June, 18). *RIT survey of Internet and at-risk behaviors* Rochester, NY:

Mead, G. (1934). *Mind, self, and society.* Chicago: University of Chicago Press.

Merriam-Webster (2010). *Power.* Retrieved December 17, 2010, from http://www.merriam-webster.com/dictionary/power

Miles, M. B., & Huberman, A. M. (1994). *Qualitative data analysis: An expanded sourcebook* (2nd ed.). Thousand Oaks, California: Sage Publications Inc.

Miller, J. (1998). Up it up: Gender and the accomplishment of street robbery. *Criminology, 37.*

Miller, J. (2001). *One of the guys: girls, gangs and gender.* New York: Oxford Press.

Miller, J. (2008). *Getting Played: African American girls, urban inequality, and gendered violence.* New York, NY: NYU Press.

Nansel, T. R., Overpeck, M., Pilla, R. S., Ruan, J. W., Simmons-Morton, B., & Sheidt, P. (2001). Bullying behaviors among US youth: Prevalence and association with psychosocial adjustment. *The Journal of the American Medical Association, 285,* 2094-2100.

National Center for Education Statistics (2009). *Indicators of school crime and safety 2007.* Retrieved August 12, 2009, from http://nces.ed.gov/programs/crimeindicators/crimeindicators2007/#top

National Center for Education Statistics (2010). *Indicators of school crime and safety: 2010.* Retrieved February 22, 2011, from http://nces.ed.gov/programs/crimeindicators/crimeindicators2010/

National Center for Education Statistics. (1993, October). *Youth indicators 1993: Trends in the well-being of American Youth* (U.S. Department of Education). Washington DC: Author.

National Center for Statistics. (2002). *Violence and discipline problems in U.S. Public School* (United States Department of Education). Washington DC: Author.

National i-SAFE Survey (2004). *National i-SAFE survey finds over half of students being harassed online.* Retrieved March 17, 2010, from http://www.isafe.org/imgs/pdf/outreach_press/Internet_bullying.pdf

Neighborhood Link (1997-2009). *14608 Zipcode Profile.* Retrieved November 9, 2009, from http://www.neighborhoodlink.com/zip/14608#economics

New York State (2010). *Governor Paterson signs the "Dignity for All Students Act".* Retrieved September 26, 2010, from http://www.state.ny.us/governor/press/090810-DignityStudentsAct.html

New York State Education Department (2010). *Guidance on bullying and cyberbullying.* Retrieved September 26, 2010, from http://www.p12.nysed.gov/technology/Internet_safety/documents/cyberbullying.html

Nicklin, K. (n.d.). *Sugar, spice, and everything nice: Raising emotionally healthy girls.* Retrieved December 5, 2010, from http://www.winnetkaalliance.org/past_articles/sugarspice.asp

Norton, D. (1978). *The dual perspective: Inclusion of ethnic minority content in the social work curriculum.* New York: Council on Social Work Education.

Olweus, D. (1993). *Bullying at School.* United Kingdom: MPG Books Ltd.

Olweus, D. (1994). Bullying at school: What we know and what we can do. *Journal of Child Psychology and Psychiatry, 35,* 1171-1190.

Olweus, D. (1999). *The nature of school bullying: A cross-sectional perspective.* Florence, KY: Routledge.

Oswald, K., Safran, S., & Johanson, G. (2005). Preventing Trouble: Making Schools Safer Places Using Positive Behavior Supports. *Education & Treatment of Children, 28*(3), 265-278.

Owens, L., Shute, R., & Slee, P. (2000). Guess what I just heard: Indirect aggression among teenage girls in Australia. *Aggressive Behavior, 26,* 67-83.

Patchin, J., & Hinduja, S. (2007). Offline consequences of online victimization: School violence and delinquency. *Journal of School Violence, 6,* 89-112.

Patchin, W. J., & Hinduja, S. (2006). Bullies move beyond the schoolyard: A preliminary look at cyberbullying. *Youth Violence and Juvenile Justice, 4,* 80-97.

Pew Research Center (2010). *Mobile access 2010.* Retrieved July 10, 2010, from http://pewInternet.org/reports/2010/mobile-access-2010.aspx

Pew/Internet and American Life Project (2007). *Teens and Social Media* (). : .

Phillips, C. (2003). Who's who in the pecking order?. *British Journal of Criminology, 43,* 710-728.

Rainwater, L. (1970). *Behind the ghetto walls: Black families in a federal slum.* Chicago: Aldine.

Raskauskas, J., & Stolz, A. (2007). Involvement in traditional and electronic bullying among adolescents. *Developmental Psychology, 43,* 564-575.

Renfro, J., Huebner, R., Callahan, C., & Ritchey, B. (2003). Violent behaviors in rural and urban school. *Journal of School Violence, 2,* 111-122.

Rhodes, B. N. (2009). Change the subject: Resilience, resistance and representation of Black adolescent females (Master's Thesis, Columbia College, 2009). *Masters Abstracts International,* 1-34.

Rice, F. P., & Dolgin, K. G. (2008). *The adolescent development, relationships, and culture* (12th ed.). United States of America: Pearson.

Richard, R., Deci, M., & Edward, L. (2000). Self-determination theory and the facilitation of intrinsic motivation, social development, and well-being. *American Psychologist, 55,* 68-78.

Rochester City School District (2009). *Districtwide official suspension report.* Retrieved March 28, 2011, from http://www.rcsdk12.org/19731052091526163/lib/19731052091526163/Yr%20End%20Official%20 Enrollment%20Rpts/08-09_Suspension_Rpt_All.pdf

Rochester Institute of Technology (n.d.). *Samuel C. McQuade, III, PhD: A biographical sketch.* Retrieved March 14, 2010, from http://www.rit.edu/~w-cfms/downloads/McQuade%20Bio%20July%202009.pdf

Rosen, L. D. (2006). *Adolescents in MySpace: Identity formation, friendship, and sexual predators.* Unpublished doctoral dissertation, California State University, California.

Sampat, N., & McQuade, S. (2008). *The Encyclopedia of Cybercrime.* Westport, CT: Greenwood Press.

Schmidt, R. A., & Wrisberg, C. A. (1941). *Motor learning and performance* (2nd ed.). Champagne, IL: Human Kinetics.

School Digger (2006-2009). *Enrollment Information for Thomas Jefferson High School.* Retrieved November 9, 2011, from http://www.schooldigger.com/go/NY/schools/2475003367/school.aspx

School Violence, Weapons, Crime, and Bullying (2010). *Important school violence statistics.* Retrieved January 30, 2011, from http://www.nssc1.org/important-school-violence-statistics.html

SchoolNet, (1997, February). . *On-line newsletter.*

Shakoor, B. H., & Chalmers, D. (1986). Co-Victimization of African American Children Who Witness Violence: Effects on Cognitive, Emotional, and Behavioral Development. *Journal of the National Medical Association, 83,* 233-238.

Sharp, S. (1995). How much does bullying hurt? The effects of bullying on the personal well-being and educational progress of secondary-aged students. *Educational and Child Psychology, 12,* 81-88.

Shelton, A. J., Owens, E. W., & Song, H. (2008). An Examination of Public School Safety Measures Across Geographic Settings. *Journal of School Health, 79,* 24-29.

Shoemaker-Richards, B. (2010). *Dignity for all students act: New York's anti-bullying law.* Retrieved September 26, 2010, from http://www.suite101.com/content/dignity-for-all-students-act---new-yorks-anti-bullying-law-a283825

Simmons, R. (2002). The hidden culture of aggression in girls. *Odd girl out* (pp. 15-38). Florida: Harcourt Books.

Simon, R. J. (1975). *Women and crime.* New York: Lexington Books.

Simpson, S., & Elis, L. (1995). Doing gender: Sorting out the cast and crime conundrum. *Criminology, 33,* 47-77.

Smith, D. C., & Sandhu, D. S. (2004). Toward a Positive Perspective on Violence Prevention in Schools: Building Connections. . *Journal of Counseling and Development, 82,* 287-293.

Steiny, J. (n.d.). *Children can learn valuable lessons from time spent at play.* Retrieved December 5, 2010, from http://www.projo.com/education/juliasteiny/content/EDWATCH_09_08-09-09_E2FAPT8_v7.36f5c58.html

Sunburst Visual Media (2003). *How not to be a victim: Violence Prevention.* Retrieved January 16, 2012, from http://www.ecb.org/guides/pdf/CE_68_06.pdf

Surra, C. A., & Milardo, R. M. (1991). The social psychological context of developing relationships: Interactive and psychological networks. In *Advances in personal relationships* (pp. -). London: Jessica Kingsley Publishers Ltd.

Talbott, E., Celinska, D., Simpson, J., & Coe, M. G. (2002). "Somebody else making somebody else fight": Aggression and the social context among urban adolescent girls. *Exceptionality, 10,* 203-220.

The History Place (1996). *The Dred Scott decision.* Retrieved October 11, 2010, from http://www.historyplace.com/lincoln/dred.htm

The Law and Policy Group, Incorporated (2008). *Report on the status of Black women and girls.* New York: Gloria J. Browne-Marshall.

Thomas, A. (2007). *Youth online: Identity and literacy in the digital age.* New York: Peter Lang Publishing Inc.

Tolson, E. R., McDonald, S., & Moriarty, A. (1990). *Peer mediation among high school students: A test of effectiveness* (University of Illinois). Chicago: University of Illinois, Jane Addams School of Social Work.

U.S. Department of Commerce (1999). *Falling through the net: Defining the digital divide.* Retrieved February 13, 2011, from http://www.ntia.doc.gov/ntiahome/fttn99/contents.html

US Census Bureau (2000). *Race.* Retrieved October 16, 2010, from http://quickfacts.census.gov/qfd/meta/long_68176.htm

USDHHS (2001). *Youth violence: A report of the Surgeon General.* Retrieved September 4, 2010, from http://www.surgeongeneral.gov/library/youthviolence/default.htm

Underwood, K. M. (2003). *Social aggression among girls.* New York: Guilford Press.

Van Manen, M. (1990). *Researching lived experience: Human science for an action sensitive pedagogy.* Albany: State University of New York Press.

Van Tilburg, T. G. (1995). Delineation of the social network and differences in network size. In *Living arrangements and social networks of older adults* (pp. 83-96). Amsterdam: VU University Press.

Vardalis, J. J., & Kakar, S. (2000). Crime and the high school environment. *Journal of Security Administration, 23*(2), 37-48.

Violence (2010). In *Dictionary.com* (p. 2). http://dictionary.reference.com/browse/violence: Ask.com.

Wang, J., Iannotti, R., & Nansel, T. (2009). School bullying among adolescents in the United Sates: Physical, verbal, relational, and cyber. *Journal of Adolescent Health, 45,* 368-375.

Watkins, C., & Wagner, P. (2000). *Improving school behavior.* London: Sage.

Watkins, C., Mauthner, M., Hewitt, R., Epstein, D., & Leonard, D. (2005). School violence, school differences and school discourses. *British Educational Research Journal, 33,* 61-74.

Weiss, J. (2007). Eyes on Me Regardless: Youth Responses to High School Surveillance. *Educational Foundations, 21*(1/2), 47-69.

Willard, N. (2006). *Cyberbullying and cyberthreats: Responding to the challenge of social cruelty, threats, and distress.* Eugene, Oregon: Center for Safe and Responsible Internet Use.

Williams, K. R., & Guerra, N. G. (2007). Prevalence and predictors of Internet bullying. *Journal of Adolescent Health*, *41*, s14-s21.

Wollack, J., & Mitchell, K. (2000). *Youth Internet Safety Survey* (University of New Hampshire Crimes Against Children Research Center,).

WordiQ (2010). *Street fighting*. Retrieved December 16, 2010, from http://www.wordiq.com/definition/ Street_fighting

Xie, H., Farmer, T. W., & Cairns, B. D. (2003). Different forms of aggression among inner-city African-American children: Gender configurations, and school social networks. *Journal of School Psychology*, *41*, 355-375

Yager, T. J., & Rotheram-Borus, M. J. (2000). Social expectations among African American, Hispanic, and European American adolescents. Cross-cultural research. *The Journal of Comparative Social Science*, 283-305.

Ybarra, M., & Mitchell, K. J. (2004a). Online aggression/targets, aggressors and targets: A comparison of associated youth characteristics. *Journal of Child Psychology and Psychiatry*, *45*, 1308-1316.

Ybarra, M., & Mitchell, K. J. (2004b). Youth engaging in online harassment: Associations with caregiver-child relationships, Internet use, and personal characteristics. *Journal of Adolescence*, *27*, 319-336.

Ybarra, M., Diener-West, M., & Leaf, P. (2007). Examining the overlap in Internet harassment and school bullying: Implications for school intervention. *Journal of Adolescent Health*, *41*, 42-50.

APPENDIX A

DRAFT OF THE LETTER TO PARTICIPANTS

Paul Miller
1 Edgerton Pk.
Rochester, NY 14608
Date:

Dear Participants,

Congratulations, you have been selected to participate in this voluntary study, because it is suspected that you will have valuable insight and experiences pertaining to how cyberbullying has affected your high school experience. In order to have been selected you must have met the following criteria: a) at least age 18, b) female, c) Black, d) at least one suspension on their record, due to a conflict, and e) have a Facebook or MySpace page that is actively used. Because students are 18 parent consent is not needed, but the students will be expected to share this letter with their parents/guardians.

I have been approved by St. John Fisher College and the Rochester City School District to conduct research for my qualitative dissertation study. My study will focus on examining the experiences urban Black adolescent females describe as participants and victims of cyberbullying, and if they were victimized, what were their experiences? This study will lend a valuable perspective to scholarly research on cyberbullying; which currently does not view cyberbullying as a specific problem in urban schools.

Dates to meet with students:

Overview Meeting: On Thursday, May 19, 2011, you will be given a pass to come to room 215 computer lab starting at 11:30. The students will meet with the researcher one on one for approximately 15 minutes each to discuss the study, complete a information sheet about basic Internet and schooling experiences, and schedule an interview date.

Interview Dates: One interview per day will be conducted in one-hour increments immediately after school starting May 23, 2011, ending June 3, 2011. Makeup dates will be scheduled to following week.

Thank you so much for agreeing to participate in this research study. Please see me in my office if you have any further questions.

Paul Miller

APPENDIX B

INITIAL MEETING SCRIPT

Congratulations, you have been selected to participate in this voluntary study, because it is suspected that you will have valuable insight and experiences pertaining to how cyberbullying has affected your high school experience. In order to have been selected you must have met the following criteria: a) at least age 18, b) female, c) Black, d) at least one suspension on their record, due to a conflict, and f) have a Facebook or MySpace page that is actively used. Because students are 18 parent consent is not needed, but the students will be expected to share this letter with their parents/guardians.

- You were previously provided with an overview letter. If you have any questions, I can answer them before we continue.

- Since all your questions have been answered, please read the consent form (See Attached) and sign if you agree to voluntarily participate in this study.

- Additionally, you will be provided with counseling (See Attached) if it is needed, you have an option to accept it or not.

- Lastly, I will need you to complete a demographic profile sheet (See Attached) that asks you about your Internet access, usage, FaceBook usage, and violent or conflict-related situations.

- Thank you for participating in the initial portion of this study, the date for your one on one interview will be on _____.

APPENDIX C

STUDENT CONSENT FORM

St. John Fisher College
Ralph C. Wilson School of Education, Ed. D Program
3690 East Avenue
Rochester, New York 14618

Title of study: "Black Females in an Urban High School Environment and Their Explored Experiences with Cyberbullying"

Name(s) of researcher(s): Paul Miller

Faculty Supervisor: Dr. Dingus-Eason Phone for further information: 585-899-3852

Purpose of study: This study will focus on examining the experiences urban Black adolescent females describe as participants and victims of cyberbullying, and if they were victimized, what were their experiences? This study will lend a valuable perspective to scholarly research on cyberbullying; which currently does not view cyberbullying as a specific problem in urban schools.

I _____, agree to participate in this research study.
                (Name of Student)

This voluntary study has been explained to my parent(s) and/or guardian(s) and they said I could participate. The only person who will know about what I say or do in this study will be the person in charge of the study, Paul Miller, who I can contact at 585-202-7757 with any questions or concerns. Signing my name below means that I have read all the information on this document thoroughly, and I agree to participate in this study. If I decide to quit the study, all I have to do is notify the person in charge.

Approval of study: This study has been reviewed and approved by the St. John Fisher College Institutional Review Board (IRB).

Place of study: Jefferson High School   Length of participation: 3 weeks

Risks and benefits: The expected risks and benefits of participation in this study are explained below:

Benefits:

- Insight will provide as to how cyberbullying generates conflict, specifically among young Black females in an urban environment.

- Learn possible effects of cyberbullying on Black female's high school experience.

Risks:

- Revisiting situations that caused conflict in the past could cause negative feelings to resurface. (Counseling will be available to all participants)

Method for protecting confidentiality/privacy:

None of the data utilized will have original names attached to it. Pseudonyms will be developed for the participants and added to the DPS, interviews, field notes, and data collection process. Each participant will have an individual file with all their research information. Each file will be coded and analyzed to ultimately create a master matrix. The matrix and all documents will be stored by using a paper copy and an electronic copy. The hard copies will be filed in a home office, and the electronic copies will be on the researcher's computer; backed up by an external hard drive. Upon completion of the study, the research will be stored, and will be properly shredded at the end of a two-year period.

Your rights: As a research participant, you have the right to:

1. Have the purpose of the study, and the expected risks and benefits fully explained to you before you choose to participate.
2. Withdraw from participation at any time without penalty.
3. Refuse to answer a particular question without penalty.
4. Be informed of appropriate alternative procedures or courses of treatment, if any, that might be advantageous to you.
5. Be informed of the results of the study.

I have read the above, received a copy of this form, and I agree to participate in the above-named study.

Print name (Participant)   Signature   Date

Print name (Investigator)   Signature   Date

If you have any further questions regarding this study, please contact the researcher listed above. If you experience emotional or physical discomfort due to participation in this study, please contact the Office of Academic Affairs at 385-8034 or the Wellness Center at 385-8280 for appropriate referrals.

APPENDIX D

INFORMATIONAL FORM

REGARDING DATA COLLECTION AND PARTICIPANTS RIGHTS

- The title of this study is "Black Females in an Urban High School Environment and Their Explored Experiences with Cyberbullying"

- The researcher is Paul Miller a full-time doctoral candidate in the Executive Leadership Program at St. John Fisher College, in Rochester, NY. Additionally, the researcher is an Assistant Principal for the Rochester City School District.

- The purpose of study is to examine the experiences urban Black adolescent females describe as participants and victims of cyberbullying, and if they were victimized, what were their experiences? This study will lend a valuable perspective to scholarly research on cyberbullying; which currently does not view cyberbullying as a specific problem in urban schools.

- The four data gathering techniques that will be utilized are: a) demographic profile sheet (DPS), b) semi-structured interviews, c) field notes, and d) document collection. The data will be collected in a time period of approximately one month, to ensure the study is complete before the end of the school year.

- None of the data utilized will have original names attached to it. Pseudonyms (in lieu of real names) will be developed for the participants and added to the DPS, interviews, field notes, and data collection process.

- Students who agree to participate in this study must have met the following criteria: a) at least age 18, b) female, c) Black, d) experienced verbal or physical conflict within four years of high school, e) must have had at least one suspension on your record, and f) have a Facebook or MySpace page that is actively used.

- Participation in this study is voluntary. Students can withdraw from this study at any time, simply by notifying the researcher. There will be no penalty for withdrawing from this study.

APPENDIX E

DEMOGRAPHIC PROFILE SHEET

1. **Today's Date:** _____

2. **Student Participant's Name:** _____

3. **Pseudonym:** _____

4. **Grade Level:** _____

5. **Age:** _____

6. **Sex:** _____

Ethnicity- Circle One:

7. Black (African American) or Black (Origins from another country)

8. If from a country other than the United States please list which one: _____

Purpose of study: This study will focus on examining the experiences urban Black adolescent females describe as participants and victims of cyberbullying, and if they were victimized, what were their experiences? This study will lend a valuable perspective to scholarly research on cyberbullying; which currently does not view cyberbullying as a specific problem in urban schools.

School Related Questions

9. Current GPA: _____

10. Have you ever had an argument with another student while you have been in High School?

_____ Yes _____ No

11. Have you ever had a physical fight with another student while you have been in High School?

_____ Yes _____ No

12. Have you ever been suspended while you have been in High School, and if **yes**, briefly state why?

_____ Yes _____ No

13. Why: _____

_____

_____

_____

_____

_____

_____

Internet Usage Questions

14. When you access the Internet, please state where you are generally located. Please list the top **three** places, one being most and three being least (ex. home, school, library, friend's house, relative's house, etc.)

1. _____

2. _____

3. _____

15. How often do you use the Internet? Circle One

Daily   Often   Sometimes   Never

16. How many hours per day do you spend on the Internet? _____

What websites do you visit regularly?

1. _____

2. _____

3. _____

4. _____

5. _____

Social Networking Questions

17. Circle **All** The Social Networking Sites You Use:

AIM Pages   Badoo   Bebo   CyWorld   EarthFrisk   ECpod

FaceBook   Faves   Friendster   Grono   LiveJournal   MySpace

MyWebProfile   NetFriendships   Tagged   Windows Live Spaces   Yahoo! 360

18. In Order, List the Top Two Social Networking Cites You Visit the Most:

1. _____

2. _____

19. What do you do while you are on your favorite Social Networking site? (Circle Top Three Activities)

Gaming   Blogging   Chatting   Online Dating

Posting Comments on Your Page   Posting Comments on Others Pages

Designing Pages   Communicating with Friends   Meeting New Friends

Gossiping   Arguing   Communicating with Family

Reuniting with Individuals from your Past

20. Give an example of you do during your favorite Social Networking activity:

_____

_____

_____

_____

_____

_____

21. Has anyone from your school ever said anything hurtful to you or about you on Facebook?

_____ Yes _____ No

22. How did it make you feel? Circle One

Sad   Mad   Disrespected Ready to Curse   Ready to Fight

23. Have you ever said anything hurtful to or about someone in your school on Facebook?

_____ Yes _____ No

24. How did you know it as hurtful? Circle One

They Told Me   They Made a Hurtful Comment Back   They Threatened Me

25. How often have you deleted another student from school, from your Facebook page? Circle One

Often   Sometimes   Never   Once

26. Has another student from school ever deleted you as a friend from their page? Circle One

Often   Sometimes   Never   Once

27. How often have you been in **verbal argument** at school because of a situation on Facebook? Circle One

Often   Sometimes   Never   Once

28 Then how many of them got you in trouble at school? Circle One

0   1-3   3-5   5-10

29. How many **physical altercations** have you been in because of a situation on FaceBook? Circle One

0   1-3   3-5   5-10

30. How many at school? Circle One

0   1-3   3-5   5-10

APPENDIX F

COUNSELING AGREEMENT

Today's Date: _____

Student Participant's Name: _____

Pseudonym: _____

Your interview was conducted on _____, and you will be contacted by a counselor from the School's Student Family Support Center on _____.

The counselor will offer you a counseling appointment to discuss anything that may have troubled you as a result of your interview. If further counseling is needed after your initial appointment; a schedule will be created for re-occurring appointments as needed. If you do not feel the need to participate in counseling, you may decline the offer. Counseling can always be scheduled at a later time if the need develops.

Best **Personal** Contact Number: _____

Only if you do not want counseling:

I do not wish to be contacted by a counselor _____   _____
                                              (Initial)   (Date)

If I later change my mind, I understand I can contact the researcher directly to arrange counseling.

_____
(Initial)

APPENDIX G

SEMI-STRUCTURED INTERVIEW QUESTIONS

Today's Date: _____

Student Participant's Name: _____

Pseudonym: _____

Purpose of study: This study will focus on examining the experiences urban Black adolescent females describe as participants and victims of cyberbullying, and if they were victimized, what were their experiences? This study will lend a valuable perspective to scholarly research on cyberbullying; which currently does not view cyberbullying as a specific problem in urban schools.

Introduction - Please keep the school setting as the basis for your answers; you can pull from this week or anytime in high school career.

1. Describe your online "Swagger/Identity" (Please provide five words that help define your online swagger)

2. How is your online Identity or "Swagger" different than your swagger at school?

3. Are you popular online?

4. How do you know you are popular online?

5. In what ways has Social Networking increased your popularity at school?

6. How does popularity online and being popular in school relate? What are three typical comments you get on your page?

7. In what ways are FaceBook friends different than real world friends?

8. How many of your FaceBook friends do you hang with in school?

9. Describe a situation where an online conflict has caused you to lose a friendship.

10. Have you ever been made to feel bad because of something someone said about you online? What was said?

11. During that bad experience, how did you react to what was being said online?

12. How did you react when you saw the person in school?

13. Have you ever said anything hurtful to someone online? What was said?

14. How did they react to what you said online?

15. How did they react to you in school?

16. What do you do when you get publically disrespected "punked" embarrassed online?

17. Can you describe a situation at school that caused you to get into a fight or an argument?

18. Have you ever been afraid to come to school because of something that happened online? What made you afraid, and what were the outcomes of the situation?

19. What role has Social Networking played in your high school experience e.g. Identity, Popularity, Relationships, Conflicts, and Suspensions, etc.?

CONTACT INFO:

Dr. Paul Miller

www.urbaneeducation.com

docmiller@urbaneeducation.com

916-2DR-PAUL (916-237-7285)